The Music Industry
A Guidebook

Cecil Hale

Stanford University/Mass Media Institute
San Francisco State University
City College of San Francisco

KENDALL/HUNT PUBLISHING COMPANY
2460 Kerper Boulevard P.O. Box 539 Dubuque, Iowa 52004-0539

Copyright © 1990 by Cecil Hale, Ph.D.

ISBN 0-8403-5672-2

All rights reserved. No part of this publication may be reproduced, stored in a retrieval system, or transmitted, in any form or by any means, electronic, mechanical, photocopying, recording, or otherwise, without the prior written permission of the copyright owner.

Printed in the United States of America
10 9 8 7 6 5 4 3 2 1

Dedication

My deepest appreciation to all who helped in making this book possible. To my students and colleagues in the Music/Recording Industry Program at San Francisco State University, my colleagues in the Mass Media Institute at Stanford University and at City College of San Francisco. Thanks to my family for being so understanding and supportive and to my colleagues and great friends in the music industry for being there all these many years.

My greatest appreciation to my family: my children Jamil, Juanita, Tasha and Antoinette, and to my partner in life, Karen, ''We've only just begun.''

To all who love the music and the special magic that makes it all happen.

Contents

Preface **vii**

Acknowledgments **ix**

Record Industry Time Line **xi**

Dateline **xiii**

Chapter 1
The Beginning 1
    Tin Pan Alley 3
    A New Marketplace 4
    TOBA 4
    Race Records 5

Chapter 2
Publishing 7
    Network Radio 10

Chapter 3
Structure of the Industry 13
    The Majors 13
    Internal Structure 14
    The Independents 17

Chapter 4
Placing the Song 25
    Making the Record 25
    The Deal 26

Chapter 5
Trade Unions and Associations 29
    Industry Performance Trade Unions 30
    Trade Associations 32

Chapter 6
Record Promotion Planning **35**

Chapter 7
Charts **41**

Chapter 8
Radio **47**

    Contemporary Hit Radio   50
    Urban Contemporary   50
    Country   51
    AOR   51
    Adult Contemporary   51
    De Facto Networks   52
    Program Suppliers   53

Chapter 9
Conclusion **73**

Appendix A
Bibliography **77**

Appendix B
Glossary **79**

Appendix C
Directory of Record Companies **85**

Preface

The record industry is, in the opinion of many universities who have adopted the study of this industry as an integral part of its curriculum, and their students, who are now pursuing these studies in record numbers, a unique fascinating field of inquiry. The music industry, historically, has been many things to many people: to the aspiring artist it has been viewed as the ultimate vehicle for expression to the masses and the potential avenue to vast wealth; to the successful writer it has been the vehicle for sharing ideas with the world (and to make money in the process); to those with entrepreneurial aspirations it has been seen as an industry in every sense of the word—having the potential to generate enormous profits while at the same time fraught with financial danger; to the consumer it has been viewed as a nondescript place from where the music originates along with the attendant messages and social cues inherent in the music and the musicians. The consumer understanding of the music industry depends very much upon whom you ask about it . . . some see the industry as being MTV, VH-1, Michael Jackson Pepsi commercials, Miami Sound Machine make-up videos, Phil Collins beer commercials, Boy George costumes, and everything else in between. Others may see the industry as C.D.'s, D.A.T's, and all of the other new technological hardware which represents the "best, the brightest, the most wonderful," devices which may change their lives. Yet others view it as the vehicle for the destruction of moral values. The most interesting fact about the music industry is that it is, indeed, all of this and much more. The answer will depend very much upon whom you ask.

It has been described as being a recession proof money machine and for many years such was the case. This was the accepted financial view until the end of the seventies when the industry suddenly saw that records are vulnerable to all of the same market forces that affect other commercial enterprises.

This multi billion dollar industry has, over the last decade, been the subject of many excellent works seeking to find the common denominator for success. The summation of these studies emphatically state that this is a business, first and foremost, and, as such, has to be operated as such. The most telling sentiment to emerge from many of these studies is that in terms of predicting what the next hit records will be, anyone's guess is as good as anyone else's; in other words this is still a business of calculated guesses . . . there is no formula for predicting hits.

The business aspect of the music industry bears a striking resemblance to any other major financial enterprise: driven by the bottom line, seeking to make the most profit from the least investment, executives who must be able to speak the language of finance as well as promotion, and the constant need of artists and material to fuel the machine. It is with this aspect in mind that this book has been written; to attempt and give students who are the aspiring executives, artists, managers, writers, and promotion persons with a small guide as to how the industry operates. This book will examine the industry from several practical points of view. By examining the industry the student will, hopefully, begin to see that, it does, indeed, behave as other enterprises in that the demonstrated behavior occurs in cycles. The most difficult part of any journey is understanding the lay of the land. This, hopefully, will be of assistance in understanding the terrain.

Acknowledgments

I wish to thank the following companies and individuals for their valuable assistance:

Stanford University, San Francisco State University Music/Recording Industry Program, and City College of San Francisco.

Dr. Henry Brietrose, Jules Dundes, Dr. Jeremy Cohen, John Newhagen, Michael Basil, Dr. Sherman Beverly,

Capitol Records, Inc., Polygram Records, Inc., Warner Brothers Records, Unlimited Gold Records, Irwin Steinberg, Bhaskar Mennon, Rupert Perry, Larkin Arnold, Don Zimmerman, Arnie Holland, Barry White, Chris Jones, Ned Shankman, Larry Thompson, Thomas Crenshaw, Joseph Porter, Bobbi Mallory, Mary Pieratt, Holly Tiegard, Augie Bloom, Earnie Singleton, Ron Ellison, Cecil Holmes, Ray Harris, Richard Egizzi, Joe Robinson, Stan Hoffman, Kenneth Gamble, and Thom Bell.

Walter Love Shaw and Radio and Records magazine, Jean Williams formerly of Billboard magazine, Jack Gibson and The Rapper magazine, Bill Gavin publications and The Gavin Report, Bob Long and Cashbox magazine and Claude Hall formerly of Billboard magazine,

Special lifelong thanks to Lucky Cordell, Rodney Jones, Steve Rivers and Jack Silver, Abe Thompson, Thomas Crenshaw, Esq.

Bill and Carol Clark . . . Thanks.

Record Industry Time Line

Event

1877 Edison patents the Phonograph.

1899 Establishment of first Majors; Columbia Phonograph Manufacturing Company.

1900 Victor Talking Machine Company. First system of record distribution through dealer network.

1910 Establishment of first performing rights society ASCAP(1914). Establishment of TOBA.

World War I

1920 Independent Record Companies proliferate.

Mamie Smith's "Crazy Blues" becomes big hit thus beginning the industry's recognition of the profitable 'race record' market.

Independent manufacturing and distribution established to service indie companies.

Field Recording centers and sessions in Atlanta and Memphis.

Establishment of Network Radio

A T and T launches first multiple station connection.

Radio Corporation of America establishes NBC.

United Independent Broadcasters becomes CBS.

Jack L. Cooper begins time brokerage broadcasting in Chicago.

RCA acquires Victor Talking Machine Company.

Stock Market Crash

1930 Independent record companies wiped out. Major companies consolidate and acquire assets of indies.

Establishment of WPA Arts Project supplies work for musicians and writers.

Proliferation of the jukeboxe creates demand for phonorecords. Discount records introduced by Decca Columbia Phonograph acquired by CBS.

World War II

1940 NAB establishes BMI in response to royalty dispute with ASCAP; A F of M calls strike against radio networks;

Single artist performances become important thus establishing a star system.

CBS labs perfect long play 33 1/3 disc format/ RCA develops 45 7" disc format. An industry format standard conflict ensues which results in both formats becoming accepted industry standards.

Network Television begins regular broadcast schedule.

1950 Introduction of Format Radio.

First *American Bandstand* broadcast.

Civil Rights Movement.

Payola investigation

1960 Folk music becomes important w/ hootenannys.

Escalation of the Vietnam Conflict. Student activism on college campuses.

San Francisco 'Be-In' Festival attracts thousands of 'flower children'. Haight-Ashbury becomes spiritual center of peace movement.

Tom Donahue begins underground format radio in San Francisco.

Woodstock Music Festival in upstate New York attracts 500,000.

1970 Payola investigation of criminal influence in records and radio.

Disco Music dominates charts FM radio bec dominates the audience ratings.

1980 Record Industry suffers severe economic decline.

Advent of digital technology with the introduction of the compact disc and players.

Introduction of MTV cable tv music channel.

Michael Jackson's *Thriller* sells 35 million and aids in reviving a stagnant industry.

1990

Dateline

1877	Thomas Edison and John Kruesi manufacture and patent the gramophone
1881	Chinster Bell and Charles Tainter improve Edison's device with reusable wax cylinders
1887	Emile Berliner patents the flat disc recording system
1889	Coin operated battery powered players introduced by Louis Glass
1890	Berliner forms the United States Gramophone Company
1891	Columbia Phonograph Manufacturing Company formed
1896	American Federation of Musicians union founded in Indianapolis, Indiana
1901	Eldredge Johnson with Berliner form the Victor Talking Machine Company and develop extensive dealer distribution network
1905	The Odeon Company of Germany introduces double-sided flat disc record
1906	Introduction of the Victrola player with speaker horn
1914	ASCAP formed in New York
1917	National Music Publishers Assn formed
1920	KDKA, Pittsburgh, becomes first commercially licensed radio station
1920	Mamie Smith becomes first solo black singer to be recorded. Her record 'Crazy Blues'. Record's success launches the 'race' records market.
1921	Harry Pace Phonograph Company formed in Harlem, New York and becomes nation's first minority owned record company
1922	A T and T begins first radio network
1922	Broadcasters form NAB
1922	Chicago's Paramount Record Company begins effective mail order business with race records
1925	Brunswick Record Co. begins sale of electric phonograph
1925	Industry establishes field recording centers in Atlanta, Ga. and Memphis, Tn.
1926	N.B.C. formed by RCA
1927	C.B.S. radio network formed by Arthur Judson
1927	Formation of the Harry Fox Agency for issuance of mechanical licenses
1928	Columbia Phonograph purchased by CBS

1928	Victor purchased by Radio Corporation of America and becomes RCA-Victor
1928	William Lear introduces the car radio
1929	Stock Market Crash spells economic disaster for country and the industry
1931	Formation of SESAC performing rights organization
1934	Government legislation creates the Federal Communications Commission
1935	Jukeboxes represent majority of record sales
1935	Under F.D.R.'s 'New Deal', the W.P.A. Arts Project helps keep the industry alive
1939	Television introduced by RCA at New York World's Fair
1940	AFM calls strike against record industry
1940	BMI formed by broadcasters through NAB in reaction to fee dispute with ASCAP
1941	First commercially licensed FM radio station
1941	World War II slows market growth as shellac, the primary manufacturing ingredient of phonorecords, is declared essential to war effort and rationed
1942	First Gold Record Award given to Glenn Miller
1945	End of war signals beginning of tremendous growth of independent companies
1945	John Mullin demonstrates German Magnetophone which begins the era of magnetic tape recording
1946	G.E. introduces the clock radio
1946	Record 'One Stops' begin operation
1948	AMOA formed to represent operators of jukeboxes
1948	CBS labs and Peter Goldmark introduces vinyl 33 1/3 rpm long playing record
1948	First network television broadcast
1948	RCA introduces 45 rpm 7" vinyl record
1952	Alan Freed begins Moon Dog program on WJW in Cleveland
1952	Bandstand television show begins in Philadelphia
1952	RIAA formed in New York
1953	Todd Storz and Gordon Mclendon begin Top 40 radio format
1954	Capitol Records purchased by England's EMI Corporation
1954	Rack Jobbers emerge as significant music merchandisers
1955	First record club formed by CBS
1955	NATRA formed to represent black radio announcers
1957	NARAS formed in Los Angeles
1957	Stereo records introduced to market by EMI and Audio Fidelity Co.
1958	8 track recorder/player introduced

1958	First Grammy Award given.
1958	Formation of NARM
1959	Congressional hearings led by Oren Harris launch payola investigation. Pay for play makes a Federal crime
1961	Satellite communication technology introduced
1962	Transistor radios introduced
1964	Beatles begin 'British Invasion' of popular music
1964	Cassette recorder/player introduced
1964	Folk music movement reaches peak
1967	Gulf and Western acquires Paramount
1967	Tom Donahue begins AOR format at KMPX in San Francisco
1969	Woodstock music festival attracts 500,000 fans
1973	Germany' Phillips and Siemens, (Polygram) acquires MGM, Mercury, and Polydor
1974	Payola investigation
1975	Record supermarkets begin to flourish
1976	First Platinum Record awards given by RIAA
1978	Disco Era begins
1979	Digital technology introduced by Phillips and SONY corporations
1979	Industry faces economic recession
1980	U.K.'s Thorn Industries acquires 50% interest in EMI forming Thorn-EMI
1981	FM radio becomes dominant music delivery system
1981	MTV launched by Warner-Amex cable
1982	Consumer compact disc players go on sale
1983	Industry begins economic recovery
1985	Industry faces yet another payola investigation regarding independent
1985	PMRC organization launches campaign for cleaner lyrics in records
1985	VH-1 begins broadcasting
1986	D.A.T. technology introduced
1987	Germany's Bertelson Music Group acquires RCA Records
1988	Japan's SONY Corporation purchases CBS Records
1989	Companies stop issuing vinyl promotional records to radio; instead c.d.'s are used
1989	Warner Communications merges with Time, Inc.
1989	Polygram acquires A & M records

Chapter 1

The Beginning

In tracing the beginnings of the popular music industry there is usually a controversy as to when this date must be assessed. It must be considered weather to date this history from the invention of the phonograph or from the beginning of the music publishing industry. In the United States these two times/events have become an integral interwoven part of today's industry. If this date is to be the beginning of publishing in the U.S. then the date would be 1640. This was the year the *Bay Psalm Book* was published in the colonies and profits realized from the sales. There obviously were no record players at this time in history but this date is important for, in examining the industry, certain bench-marks of success become evident; the indicators for each era have always been measured in commercial terms—did it make money.

The beginning of the record industry is acknowledged as the date of the invention of the phonograph. This device, the invention of Thomas Edison and the Edison Labs in New Jersey, was patented in 1877 but the commercial impact of this invention to the world of music would not be seen for several years. Edison did not originally intend his machine to be, primarily, a musical instrument. His initial idea was to use this device as a dictation machine to help speed office work, to preserve the valuable artifacts of our heritage for posterity, to facilitate learning and hundreds of other noble intentions. The phonograph, or more properly, gramophone, was a simple, yet, brilliant idea. Edison's theory stated that it was possible to capture sound; to reduce sound into a physical, tangible form; to produce a physical pattern that would be analogous to the sound pattern of the originating sound source in order to store this sound for later listening. His method was, by today's standards, very basic but, as history would prove, a very durable one. Edison's device used a strip of tinfoil attached to a rotating cylinder. This cylinder was rotated by a hand cranked mechanism geared to cause the cylinder to turn at a constant speed. Above the foil was the actual transducing element, the device used to convert the physical sound waves into a mechanical representation. Edison's primary *element* was a moving diaphragm microphone attached to a sapphire stylus. As a person spoke into a microphone, the pressure from the resulting sound wave caused a displacement of a diaphragm. This movement caused the stylus to indent the foil in direct proportion to the strength and frequency of the sound wave resulting in a groove being cut into the foil that was a physical picture of the sound wave

. . . an *analog*. The playback process was the exact reverse. As the stylus moved along the groove and the indentations it would move in direct proportion to the size of the indentation. This in turn would cause the diaphragm attached to the stylus to vibrate thus creating sound waves.

Even though the quality of the sound was inadequate by today's standards, Edison's idea of analog recording would remain unchanged until the 1980's and the advent of digital electronics. All other ideas for disc recording from the 1880's until the 1980's were simply improvements to the analog recording/playback theory of Edison. Edison also goes down in history as the first recording artist, as the first recording made was of Edison reciting 'Mary had a little Lamb.'

Over the next several years following the introduction of Edison's patented machine there were several improvements to Edison's system which included changing the cylinder from tin foil to wax so as to make them reusable. However the first major change did not occur until the advent of disc recording.

This technology of cylinder recording was dominant until the invention of the *flat disc recording process*. This technique, developed by Emile Berliner and Eldridge Johnson, would also prove to be very durable over time. Berliner, a researcher at Bell laboratories, was astute in the ways of business as well as the world of electronics. He and Johnson established the Victor Talking Machine company in January 1901 to capitalize upon this idea. What made this technology especially exciting (and profitable) was the ability to make duplicates of these recordings, a difficult feat for the Edison machines. With the flat disc machines and the establishment of the Victor Company to capitalize upon this idea, a new development crucial to the development of the record industry was born. As the primary objective of Victor and Columbia was to sell the machines as opposed to selling the records an elaborate distribution system was developed. This network of equipment suppliers, these retail outlets for the machines would also, initially, be the outlet for the records. As these companies grew through the beginning of the century so the record industry grew.

As the phonograph was becoming a major source of American entertainment a possible concern for companies selling these machines would be to consider what Americans did for musical entertainment at the turn of the century.

The minstrel shows of the late 1800's were still very prevalent in many part of the country. Consumers in the major cities relied upon the theaters for exposure to new songs and family entertainment. It was from these shows that Americans found the 'hits' of the day which they would use in home entertainment.

Another significant aspect of the American social life was the player piano. For the well heeled and cultured of the late 1800's and the early 1900's a piano in the parlor for entertaining friends and family was not unusual. If these families were really current with the new technology, they would own a player piano. These pianos had the ability to play back music from a pre-recorded, or more properly, a pre-cut roll. These rolls were produced by publishing houses which granted licenses to manufacturers to duplicate these rolls for distribution. The parallel between the manufacturing and duplication of the piano roll and the subsequent manufacturing and distribution of phono-records becomes, historically, apparent. The licensing process became the same. Piano rolls and phonorecords today still fall into the same copyright classification as defined by the U.S. Government.

Tin Pan Alley

The musical shows and musical theater were other places for music to be exposed to an audience. The center for this activity was New York City and, as such, was considered to be the musical center of the country. As shows were produced for the theater, there was an ongoing need for material, the need for a continuous supply of songs. These were supplied by the publishing industry and its songwriters. The music publishing industry, also centered in New York, was located near the theater district on Broadway and was affectionately known as *Tin Pan Alley*. As these publishers acquired songs a mechanism had to be in place to obtain exposure. This was accomplished by staff members of the various publishing houses whose primary job was to identify, meet, and convince those responsible for song placement in other shows to use these songs. These early promoters of music were called *song pluggers*. Each song plugger was, of course, in direct competition with other pluggers from the publishing houses which meant that the song pluggers life was high pressure and highly competitive. His fortunes, along with those of his employer, rose and fell based on the number of songs placed. As there usually was room for only a limited number of songs and there was the aspect of some producers producing their own songs i.e . . . George M. Cohan, the song plugger had to be aggressive, inventive and in some cases unethical. Certain song pluggers were not beyond using money and other forms of inducement to persuade the producer to include his songs in the repertoire. (Clark 1977) The idea was that if the song were included within the show the publishing houses would profit in two ways: (1) public performance of these songs would generate revenues from ticket sales and (2) these performances translated directly into the sale of *sheet music*. Sheet music, the printed document containing the lyrics and music of a song, was the requirement for the consumer to play these songs at home on the pianos. This also meant that the publishers, who were the copyright and print producers of this music had a tremendous financial stake in the hearing and performance of their respective songs as these activities produced performance rights royalties. The song plugger/show producer combination created demand for a product, in this case the printed music. Along the way, significant performance royalties would also be generated. The direct corollary of this relationship to song placement and subsequent performance is to be found in today's record market with the record promotion person. What is at stake in this relationship is that created demand translates directly into phonorecord/tape/CD sales for the record company. The generated airplay produces significant performance royalties from radio, television, cable, and concerts. How this operates will be explained farther in the examination of music publishing.

Recorded music had become a very important entertainment and propaganda factor with the advent of World War I. During this period in American history the music industry thrived as Tin Pan Alley turned its attentions to patriotic songs. The theaters in New York continued to do extremely well with large stock shows like the Ziegfield Follies. Producers and writers like Geo. Cohan thrived during this period. It was also during this period of Prohibition, Speakeasys, and the era affectionately known as the 'Roaring Twenties' that the music industry underwent tremendous change.

A New Marketplace

In examining the show business climate, it is also of importance to understand the sociological structure of the U.S. especially those regarding race relations. In the early part of the century, civil rights was not a very high priority on the American agenda.

During the late 1800's, many American sociological changes were to aid the record and music industries. When the Civil War ended in 1865 the black population was estimated to have been approximately 4,800,000. Most of these newly freed persons were in the rural south with only approx. 488,070 of these being originally freed before the Emancipation Proclamation. With the abolition of slavery via the Emancipation Proclamation in 1863 and the addition of the 13th amendment to the United States Constitution in 1865, Black Americans were now legally free to migrate to any part of the country. A top priority for this population was to find employment as most of them were unskilled and illiterate. For many of these newly freed Americans the prospects of employment lay in the industrialized cities. This population movement after the civil war, with the shift of much of the black population during the late 1800's moving from a rural to urban industrial environment, created a new, concentrated group of potential entertainment consumers. As a result of this movement came the demand for more acts and, as the tremendous urban black population growth continued, there was now a demand for theaters to address this need.

To profit from this population shift and resulting need for entertainment venues to accommodate these 'new' consumers of music, a chain of theaters was established in the south that were segregated but available and clearly profitable to its owners. This new group of theaters, affectionately called 'Toby Time' by the Black entertainers forced to endure terrible treatment from the theater proprietors, served as the archetypal example of exploitation of black consumers and entertainers.

TOBA

In the early 1900's blacks could perform in limited segregated theaters and black theatergoers could attend these performances but had to watch from small segregated areas. By 1907 *T.O.B.A.*, the Theater Owners Booking Agency, was established to supply black acts to black theater goers. These theaters were white run offering very little in amenities to entertainers. Most entertainers had to travel at their own expense to work in very squalid conditions for little pay. Many of these entertainers were forced to use the bottom of the stage as the dressing area and, after a performance, were not given any guarantees of being paid at all. *T*ough *on B*lack *A*sses became the joke among these traveling musicians and dancers as they understood that work for them was very, very different than that given to their white counterparts in the 'serious' theaters of New York and other parts of the travelling show circuit.

Race Records

Until the 20's it was a rare occurrence for any American ethnic group other than white artists to be recorded. There was assumed to be a very small market for the recordings of Blacks in particular. This remained the accepted and operational fact until 1920. In that year the first black solo artist, Mamie Smith, was recorded for the OKEH label. The major record companies had not recorded black soloists for fear of a backlash, especially from southern retailers and consumers which the companies assumed would result in a boycott of the players each company manufactured.[1] The first company to record a black artist was the independent OKEH under the supervision of Ralph Peer. This session was actually a fluke as Mamie was intended to be a backup singer for Sophie Tucker, one of Broadway's leading stars. With all the makings of a Hollywood movie, Ms. Tucker was taken suddenly ill. Mamie stepped in, with the urging of her manager Perry Bradford. The song recorded in this historic studio session, *Crazy Blues,* became an unlikely success story for OKEH Records. OKEH, a division of the major General Phonograph Company, was understandably worried, however, these worries were soon put to rest as Smith's record sold an astonishing 75,000 copies in the first month. With the success of this initial recording of a black artist, the record industry recognized that there was significant potential profit in these specialized recordings. By 1922, the record industry was reaping the benefits of this 'new' market at the rate of five (5) million copies a year. These recordings came to be classified as Race records—records recorded by blacks and intended for a black audience. With this new success from this new market came new problems. The major problem now faced by the willing manufacturers of these records was filling the demand for talent. Phonograph retailers, part of the distribution network of these companies, became instant A and R talent scouts. Another approach companies developed to accommodate this demand for new talent was to set up *field recording centers.* These regional outposts for recording were not really outposts at all. The idea was to take the technology of recording to the talent—to create make-shift studios wherever talent could be found. These field recording centers were located in two southern cities: (1) Atlanta—intended to find and record hillbilly (country) artists and (2) Memphis—for the recording of race record artists.

As the race record market grew during the early twenties, a number of independent record companies were established to take advantage of this newfound and highly profitable trend. The Harry Pace Phonograph Corporation in New York City and its Black Swan Label was one such company. The establishment of this company also signaled another first for the recording industry as it was the first Black owned recording company. The growth of the independent record market during this period created a demand for other record industry entities namely independent record pressing plants and distributors to service the manufacturing requirements of these new companies. These independent record companies grew at an astonishing rate with the introduction of these race records. A prominent example of the success of these specialized music companies was Paramount Records of Port Washington, Wisconsin. This company had been operating since 1917 but found it's greatest success in the middle 20's with race record artists. Stars like Gertrude Rainey, one of its premier race record artists, helped make this company highly visible and profitable. An interesting aspect of Paramount's marketing strategy was the idea of using newspaper advertising for product solicitation. It was not unusual for record companies to use newspapers to sell its products but it was a novel idea for these companies to target its audience along racial lines using ethnic newspapers. Paramount's advertising in the Chicago area, directed toward a tremendous black population, was done through the *Chicago Defender*. This newspaper, one of many daily newspapers established nationally to reach the black population, was established as the journalistic voice of the black community and by the early twenties had a weekly circulation of 100,000 copies. By placing advertising in this newspaper Paramount had found a formula for promotion which was both unique and effective for the record industry. Paramount's use of the specialized print media gave it the ability to target a specific market and, by requiring advance payment for orders, the company was allowed to operate without maintaining huge inventories. Paramount was able through this mail order marketing scheme to assess exactly the number of records to be manufactured by the number of pre-paid orders. This system of 'cash up front' had several obvious benefits to the company. Coupled with an aggressive A and R policy of finding blues artists to supply the label, it operated as a tremendous success story for independent companies.

Note

1. The Devil's Music p. 92

Chapter 2

Publishing

It was also during the first few years of the 1900's that a new awareness of the power of the publishers was felt with the formation of performance rights organizations. The first of these guilds established for the benefit of songwriters was ASCAP, The American Society of Composers Authors and Publishers. ASCAP was formed in 1917 to serve as a bargaining and collection guild for publishers. One popular story regarding ASCAP's formation tells of its beginning as the reaction to songwriters being refused payments from certain users of music, primarily the hotels, clubs, and taverns of New York City. The idea of a guild came after the urging of European songwriter Guiccamo Puccini and his agent. Puccini, on a trip to New York was surprised to find that he had not acquired royalties, nor could he expect any, from the performances of his compositions in the United States. This apparently was a tremendous personal surprise to Puccini in that European composers had been receiving royalties for many years through performing rights guilds. Puccini's recommendation was that his agent and several other song publishers investigate the formation of a guild for their protection.

Copyright holders were, indeed, aware that the legal issue of payment for public performances of songs had been established in a series of unique court cases. The legal framework for these cases began with the United States Copyright Law of 1889 which proceeded from previous government guarantees of protection for printed material. This protection came from the initial U.S. Copyright Law of 1790 which stated that it was entirely proper for the owner of a song to expect payment for public performance. The problem for copyright holders then became the issue of enforcement and collection. At the initial called meeting to organize this new guild, the attendance was not as expected, however, the organizers were convinced that such an organization could and would be formed in time. It was decided that a second meeting should be called to attempt organization. At the second meeting, with a much more significant turnout, ASCAP was formed. The initial test for this new organization was to collect fees for music use from establishments in New York City and it was agreed by the members that this contribution would be called a *licensing fee* in the amount of $8.23 a month per establishment.

What resulted from this opening episode in ASCAP's history were the beginnings of the classic confrontation between those who produce the music and those who use it. According to these establishments, the initial targets of ASCAP licensing, they were in fact doing the publishers a *favor* by allowing their music to be performed. These proprietors felt that by playing the music the establishments were, in fact, creating demand which in turn promoted the sale of sheet music. ASCAP's position was quite different. ASCAP felt that it was *because* of the music that these enterprises were successful—that an establishment enjoyed larger sales when customers were allowed to hear music. ASCAP felt that by supplying the music which helped create demand for a business that the writers were defacto partners without realizing any of the profits. This, in essence, became the center of the debate. Did those who produced the music have any claim to any profits of a restaurant whose primary business was selling food even though music was an incidental part of the atmosphere in which this business occurred. What was the relationship between hotels and music, between restaurants and songs, between writers and indirect consumers? It was obvious that these issues would not be settled without defining the applicable laws of copyright and putting a mechanism in place to enforce them.

ASCAP, understanding the difficulty in collecting fees, filed suit in Federal Court. The initial verdict ruled in favor of ASCAP on the grounds of copyright infringement but also aided the users by finding that the musical materials in question for this case were not performed for profit, therefore, were in the public domain without expectation of fee payment. On ASCAP's appeal of this ruling the courts confirmed the lower court's ruling. This test case eventually reached the Supreme Court which reversed the lower courts and ruled in favor of ASCAP. The decisions in the cases heard before the Supreme Court—Herbert vs. Shaneley and Church vs. Hilliard—were clearly defined and stated that profit or not, the copyright holder must be compensated for public performances of copyrighted materials. This ruling was an astounding victory for ASCAP for it, in fact, established the foundation and defined the unlimited reach and power of copyright holders. Now armed with the legal backing of the nation's highest court ASCAP had the ammunition it needed to collect royalties.

Over the ensuing years, with the advent of network commercial radio in the middle twenties, talking movies and, ultimately, television in the late 1940's, along with other emerging forms of mass media technologies, the reach and power of ASCAP increased, for all of these were dependent on music and, as such, their use of music was public performance which meant, financially, ASCAP was a substantial force which these users had reckoned with. ASCAP, understanding the power of the license and understanding it's unique position of controlling the flow of music, continued to raise it's licensing fees.

ASCAP existed as the only performing rights organization until the formation of Broadcast Music, Inc. (BMI) by the nation's broadcasters acting through its organization, the National Association of Broadcasters (NAB) in 1941. The establishment of this new performing rights organization was a direct result of the network radio's inability to ever come to terms with ASCAP regarding performance fees. It was the broadcaster's position that ASCAP had become unreasonable in its fee structure. In negotiation sessions both sides were convinced that each was correct in visualizing the other as less than honorable. ASCAP's position was that the networks had enjoyed enormous profits as the direct result of using its music therefore was entitled not only to a fee but a percentage of all revenues derived by these companies. It was radio's position that the fees already paid were reasonable and that ASCAP was, in fact, becoming greedy. ASCAP threatened to withdraw all licenses to the networks if the two groups would or could not come to terms. Radio, fearing a music blackout and understanding that this would most certainly hurt profits, reacted by exploiting the weakness of ASCAP. ASCAP had an internal policy which rewarded older members with a greater proportion of generated fees. This inequity in fees paid to the newer members of the guild compared with those of the older, established members. What the NAB proposed was a new organization, separate from radio ownership but established by radio. BMI's appeal would be to new writers guaranteeing equal participation for all members in payment of royalties. With this proposal broadcasters had accomplished two things (1) a guarantee that the networks would not find themselves without music and (2) a new incentive for ASCAP bargaining position to be less rigid.

In 1945 with the end of World War II, the American music industry witnessed a virtual explosion of independent record companies featuring the music of new writers, many unable and unwilling to join the more rigid ASCAP. These writers, the new constituents of BMI propelled this organization to prominence and gave it new financial muscle. For many years after WWII, most notably the 50's with the explosion of rock and roll, BMI came to be viewed as the organization for new young writers, ASCAP as the organization for the old writers of the classic standards.

Today ASCAP, BMI, and a third organization SESAC are the dominant performing rights organizations in the United States. Each is highly successful and each uses a separate formula for determining how writers will be compensated for performances of their songs however they each function and serve as conduits of income from uses to the producers of the music.

During the period of 1910–1920 the record industry experienced tremendous growth. With a healthy economy, record players still very much a novelty, a wider repertory of available songs, and with the end of World War I, Americans were now spending more money for entertainment. If we add to this formula the aspect of Prohibition and the era still historically referred to as The Roaring Twenties—recklessness, devil-may-care attitudes—and fun loving attitudes it could be expected that entertainment would prosper.

Distribution for the independent companies of the '20's became a major problem as most of these small companies were selling and delivering records to dealers by methods as basic as offering records from the trunk of the owner's car. Accommodation of this new crop of independent record companies was addressed by the formation of a network of independent distribution companies. The major problems the independent distributors faced was the same as the very companies they existed to serve: limited capital which meant caution was required for every record signed. These companies were, quite understandably, interested in carrying those items which would have immediate salability which also meant that every record offered to them by these independent record companies was not accepted.

This cautious approach translated into an arrangement of record-by-record deals with independent companies. For the independent record company owner every record became a project to sell the distributor first, and with distribution deals being signed on a record by record basis. (expand)

The record industry, driven by successes of specialty market records, became highly profitable during the early twenties. The only perceived threat, as seen by the recording companies to this new era of profitability, was the emergence of the new technology of radio.

Network Radio

Commercial network radio became a reality in 1923 with American Telephone and Telegraph Company forming the first link between two broadcast stations. It is interesting that one of the first uses of radio, as envisioned by AT & T, was a city-wide pay device. What AT & T envisioned was a studio looking much like a telephone booth. Consumers anxious to reach a party would deposit coins in this booth which would give the consumer immediate access to a radio transmitter for a limited time and the consumers message would be broadcast. This idea did not catch on in a big way but it did prove that consumers would be willing to *pay* for services involving radio. The event which confirmed these findings was the first commercial—a ten minute broadcast paid for by a New York reality company on AT & T's WEAF.

The formula of networking, connecting two or more stations to carry simultaneous broadcasts, came into its maturity with the establishment of the National Broadcasting Company radio network. NBC, established in 1926, began as the broadcasting subsidiary of the Radio Corporation of America (RCA) which itself began as a joint venture with General Electric and Westinghouse and the divestiture of the American Marconi company by the U.S. government. American Marconi, a division[1] of British Marconi, had become highly successful in the broadcasting of wireless communications. It was during WW I that American Marconi encountered difficulties for the American government. These began when Marconi wanted to charge high rates for the transmission of high priority government war related messages. A movement resulted within the Department of the Navy with the then Secretary of Commerce Herbert Hoover that said that American defense was at the mercy of a foreign company. Thus began the movement to dismantle American Marconi, the development of a American defense communication system, and the formation of domestic communication companies whose authority would proceed from the Department of Commerce. The network became highly successful and as a result of the stations acquired from AT & T established a second branch which in reality was a second network. NBC's Red and Blue networks remained the country's only two national radio services until the advent of the third commercial network, which came into existence in 1927 as the United Independent Broadcasting Company which ultimately became CBS the Columbia Broadcasting System. United Independent, which had formed a network of 12 stations, with WOR in New York as its flagship station, needed and secured financial backing from a recording company.

The recording industry, which viewed network radio as a threat to its profitability, adopted the strategy of corporate participation thus the Columbia Phonograph manufacturing company, a major, invested in United independent and became its partner charged with the responsibility of generating network sales. This marriage of companies proved to be very unprofitable and the network was sold in 1928 to William S. Paley for $ 400,000.

Network radio rarely used recorded music for several reasons: the technical quality of the recordings was far below that of live bands and the musicians union's (A F of M) reluctance to allow recorded music. The union's concern was job security for its members, who now were needed by the networks to supply the music between the variety shows and vaudeville acts which had now moved to this medium. As historical aside, the successful RCA acquired the Victor Talking Machine Company in 1929.

The recorded music industry, concerned with the potential impact radio might have upon the sale of records and the machines on which these records were played looked upon network radio as the enemy. The record industries response to this perceived threat became an effort by the majors to share in ownership. The Columbia Phonograph company formed a partnership with United Independent Broadcasters in 1927 to act as its sales agent. The Victor Talking Machine Company became a subsidiary of The Radio Corporation of America and came to be known as RCA-Victor.

The record industry continued its growth throughout the twenties fueled by a growing economy, radio, new recording stars, and the public's willingness to have fun but disaster was just around the corner.

In 1929 and the crash of the stock market, the record industry found itself in the position of trying to survive. 1930, the worse year in dollar amounts for the industry, saw the virtual elimination of all independent companies, the consolidation of the majors, and marketing innovation as the industry struggled to survive. With consumer demand all but destroyed and the public's need for players and records overshadowed by its need of food and jobs, the record industry found its salvation in two very different places. The first was the changing of American listening habits . . . not in taste but in location. As clubs went out of business, the neighborhood tavern became the new place to congregate. These local pubs relied upon recorded music for its clients and this need was filled by the jukebox. Jukeboxes, by purchasing records, are given credit with saving the industry from the troubled years between 1930–1934. The other saving grace for the record industry was the U.S. government.

In recovering from the depression, Americans had installed a new president, Franklin Roosevelt, who promised the country a fresh start—A New Deal—as his social reform program was known. Part of the New Deal was the formation of the WPA, the Works Projects Administration which was the governments attempt to put America back to work with the government as the largest employer. Under the banner of the WPA was the Arts Project, whose job was to supply funds to artists in order to preserve the country's cultural heritage. Under this scheme, writers were paid to continue the creation of songs and musicians were paid to perform at government funded functions. The publishing houses, the primary employers of writers, were funded to keep writers working. The songs created under this arrangement belonged, of course, to the publishing houses who, in turn were compensated each time these songs were publicly performed thus insuring continued profits for the publishers.

In the 1940's the industry found itself, again, in a state of arrested growth with the advent of WWII. The main concern of the manufacturers of music during this period was the government materials restriction which mandated that records could only be purchased when additional records were turned in by consumers, thus assuring a balance in materials expended. This restriction kept control of the industry, primarily in the hands of the majors until the end of the war in 1945.

After WWII and the lifting of the materials restriction, the industry experienced an explosion of independent record companies with the majority of them specializing in race records. As these industries grew, the volume of records sold grew at a never before seen pace.

During the late 40's with the advent of CBS's long playing 33 1/3 12" album and RCA's 45 rpm 7" single record, the industry now had the ideal formats for presenting single and repertorial performances.

In the '50's the industry experienced another period of growth as the young American culture, considered rebellious against authority and flush with disposal dollars, fueled an industry that was now gearing itself toward rock and roll. The impact of format radio with the top 40 format in the early '50's, the movie industry's involvement with this youth culture, and the success of Black records now called rock and roll, the success of Elvis Presley, the incorporation of television into the youth formula with American Bandstand, changes in technology with transistor radios, stereo records, and economic good times caused the industry's growth to continue at a phenomenal rate.

The 60's saw Vietnam, Woodstock, folk music, Motown, The Beetles, Aretha Franklin, Black pride, country and western become Country, The Graduate, Haight-Ashbury, the Civil Right's movement, and general social upheaval. The sixties also saw independent record companies thrive.

The '70's saw Saturday Night Fever, Disco's, Peter Frampton, and the unprecedented growth of the majors as they consolidated to become mega-giants.

The '80's saw economic chaos, Michael Jackson, MTV, VH-1, and the majors consolidate even more to almost total control of the industry.

All in all, the music industry, now a multi-billion dollar business, continues to grow and, as such, continues to become even more complex. It is from this vantage point that we begin our journey.

Note

1. Television, Radio and Society pp. 27.

Chapter 3

Structure of the Industry

Structure of the Industry

The recording industry is comprised of companies, organizations whose primary business is the making and selling of phonorecords in every conceivable configuration. These organizations are classified according to size and degree of function into either major or independent record companies. The majors are those corporate giants who virtually control the industry. The independents are the smaller companies not affiliated with any major company. It is not always a good barometer to measure if a company is a major or independent by gross revenues for in several instances there are independent companies whose operations and profits resemble those of the majors but they still remain independents. Notable examples include Motown Records, the most successful of the independents in the late 60's and 70's and A and M, a highly successful company whose operation would rival any major operation.

The Majors

In investigating the music industry it is of vital importance to understand the players. In the game of record manufacturing in the United States there are six (6) main players that control eighty-five per cent (85%) of the record market. These very large companies, 'the big six', are the major recording empires. Major record companies are generally identified by the following characteristics: 1. Usually a very large organization with specialized departments, 2. Has tremendous financial resources, 3. Has its own distribution system and network, 4. Has its own manufacturing facilities, 5. Usually has its own studios, 6. Usually is affiliated with international companies of the same name and under the same corporate umbrella.

 (1) **C.B.S. Records, Inc.**—CBS began as the Columbia Phonograph Manufacturing Company a few years before the turn of the century. C.B.S. Records, Inc. is currently the largest of the domestic majors. CBS's holdings include the Columbia label, the EPA associated labels, a branch distribution network, April/Blackwood publishing, a mail order record club, and a network of manufacturing facilities. The CBS Records Group was sold by the parent cooperation, CBS, Inc., in 1988 to the Sony Corporation of Japan. This sale became one of the

largest financial transactions in the history of the music industry. What made this deal so appealing to the Sony Group were the vast holdings and catalogue of this giant company.

(2) **Capitol/EMI Thorn, Inc.**—Capitol Records located in Hollywood, Ca. was started as an independent company after World War II by Johnny Mercer. Capitol was later sold to the U.K. conglomerate of EMI and in 1980 the Capitol/EMI combine was fifty (50%) acquired by the U.K. Thorn Group. Capitol's holdings include Capitol Records, Inc, United Artists Records, EMI America, Screen Gems Publishing, a branch distribution network, and manufacturing facilities.

(3) **WEA, Inc.**—WEA is Warner Brother Records which began as an independent label in the '50's, Elektra Records which began as a folk music label in 1949 in New York City and Atlantic Records which began as an independent rhythm and blues specialty label in 1948. The WEA combine is owned by Warner Communications which is owned by the Kinney Corporation. WEA's holdings include a branch distribution network, pressing and manufacturing facilities, publishing interests, and label affiliations.

(4) **RCA Records**—RCA, based in New York City, began as the Victor Talking Machine Company in 1901 until its eventual acquisition by the Radio Corporation of America in 1925. RCA was purchased in 1986 by the Bertelson Music Group. RCA's holdings include a branch distribution network, publishing interests and manufacturing facilities.

(5) **Polygram Records**—Polygram, USA based in New York City is a division of the Polygram Worldwide Music Group based in Hamburg, Germany and Baarne, The Netherlands. Mercury Records, an integral part of the Polygram empire, began in Chicago in 1946 as an independent company The Polygram USA records group includes Phonogram/Mercury records, Polydor, Casablanca records, Polygram Distribution, Inc., a branch distribution system, manufacturing facilities and publishing interests.

(6) **MCA Records**—MCA Records, based in Studio City, Ca. is part of the giant MCA Entertainment Complex. MCA began originally as a talent booking agency, the Music Corporation of America. MCA Records is owned by the MCA Corporation which also owns Universal Studios and Universal Pictures. MCA Records' greatest strength until the middle '80's was its distribution network.

Internal Structure

Record companies are divided into job-intensive departments, each charged with doing a specific job in the coordinated effort to make and sell records. Each department is an island unto itself yet must function much like a gear in a machine if the machine is to work. Each department is expected to be very aggressive in its specific area of interest yet not operate as a separate company. These departments are:

(1) **A and R**—A and R stands for Artists and Repertoire. This department is responsible for talent acquisition. As the lifeblood of any company is the acts that are signed and produced, A and R becomes a vital function. This department is usually headed by a Senior Vice-President and, in major record companies is further subdivided into specialized divisions—each charged with talent acquisition in its area. A major company may have one or several A and R executives for country, rock, urban contemporary, pop, classical, jazz, etc. Each of these divisions, usually headed by a vice-president, reports to the senior A and R executive who ultimately reports to the president of the company. A and R is also responsible for pairing artists with producers, for aiding in song selection, for determining the sequence of songs on projects, and for overseeing the production budgets.

(2) **Promotion**—The promotion department is responsible for getting the company's product seen and heard. What this means is that the promotion personal are concerned with, primarily, obtaining radio and television airplay. The majority of record consumers make the decision to purchase a record by hearing the record via radio. The promotion executive has to be part salesman, part pitchman, part radio programmer, and part magician. When it is considered that every record company is approaching radio stations for airplay this makes the promotion person's job highly competitive. The promotion person is also responsible for generating chart numbers by reporting to the trade magazines a record's activity on an almost daily, most certainly a weekly basis. The promotion department in a large record company is usually headed by a Senior Vice-President. Promotion is, as are other departments, subdivided into specialized promotion units i.e. Pop, Urban, Country, AOR, etc. Each division is usually headed by a vice-president who serves as the general manager of the field personnel. Promotion field persons are usually assigned territories and based in branches serving these areas. These regions of the country are his/her responsibility. They usually service the radio and television stations within that region by bringing them the newest company releases along with information to convince the station programmer that this product would be good for their station.

Promotion persons are also assigned other duties defined by markets they are trying to reach. These markets are further specialized which define even more the job description of promotion specialists. It is possible to find a promotion person responsible for college radio promotion, another for smaller, secondary and tertiary, radio markets, yet another for.... The promotion department must also operate with a plan of coordinated airplay for the trade magazines measure a record's success based on its weekly performance The promotion department is, again, critical for the success of the record company. A recent addition to many promotion departments is a promotion specialist for video. As television plays a greater role in a company's promotion strategy, a person is required to service this segment. This new relationship with television has continued to grow as television's influence in the selling of records has grown. However, the promotion department still has to concentrate on delivering radio, still the number one way by which consumers hear new music.

(3) **Publicity**—This department is responsible for maintaining a relationship with the press—the newspapers and magazines—and any other organization who can help spread the 'gospel' about an act. The publicity department also acts as an institutional 'evangelist', responsible for putting the company's best foot forward. This department is usually headed by a vice-president and is rarely subdivided into specialized areas.

(4) **Sales**—The sales department has the responsibility of monitoring a record's progress at the wholesale and retail level. The sales department's job includes soliciting and taking orders for product, identifying retailers for point of purchase sales materials i.e. posters, billboards etc., convincing wholesale and retail merchants to buy records in quantity, and otherwise aiding these merchants in their sales efforts. The sales department is usually headed by a vice-president who manages sales personnel throughout the company's branch structure. The sales department also recommends discount and credit policies for the company. Sales, in most cases, follows the lead of promotion with new records. When a record is added to a radio or television station play list in a market, the sales department priority is that records are available for consumer purchase. The sales department is also responsible for determining the number of records actually needed in a market so as not to make the supply exceed demand. To order too many records would start a chain reaction of the manufacturing plants spending too much time producing records which may never be sold, etc. (amplify)

(5) **Marketing**—This department insures that support material is provided to aid the efforts of promotion and sales. Marketing is responsible for designing commercial campaigns, obtaining radio and television commercial advertisement, placing commercial ads in newspapers and magazines, authorizing co-op (shared) advertising with retailers, and other support activities to insure the company's message is heard by the consumer. Marketing also oversees merchandising activities in designing sales aids.

(6) **Creative Services**—Creative Services handles album cover design, poster design, record inner sleeve design, and other aspects of a project which require visual aids. This department, in conjunction with the artist, promotion, A and R, sales, and marketing, develops visual concepts to make a record jacket much more than packaging. Since album jackets border, in some cases, with art, the person in charge of this department usually has artistic training.

(7) **Business Affairs**—This department is usually staffed by lawyers for it is this department's responsibility to negotiate and supervise the writing and execution of contracts. The personnel within this department are entrusted by the company

to understand the financial implications of every contract and to insure that all terms are reasonable, favorable to the company, and that they will be honored.

(8) **Manufacturing**—This department, usually a division, is responsible for the general operations required to physically make the finished record, tape, single record, or whichever configuration is required to have a finished product. Manufacturing is also responsible for insuring that the manufacturing plants are operating at capacity.

(9) **Branches**—These are the company's distribution "outposts", regional offices responsible for carrying out the mandates of the national company policy staff while having a knowledge of the markets they serve. These are usually managed by Branch Managers who report to the Vice-Presidents of Marketing and Sales and ultimately to the President. Within each branch are local salespersons and other support personnel for areas like merchandising.

The Independents

There are other companies which vie for the remaining 15% of the national record market. These companies are called independents. These companies range in size from the smallest cottage industry operations to the very large companies which look very much like majors.

There are an uncountable number of independent music production companies as, one of the characteristics of the indie is a lack of need for massive manpower. Independent companies are identified by the following characteristics:

1. Usually a small organization with limited manpower.
2. Has limited financial resources.
3. Does not own its distribution system.
4. Does not own its manufacturing facilities.
5. Usually does not own its own studios.
6. Is not a branch of any other major company.

Independent companies usually cannot supply all of the same services as a major company and usually rely upon the majors, via various deals, to supply needed services. One such proposition is the pressing and distribution deal (P and D). Under this arrangement, the independent will affiliate with a major and its manufacturing facilities to produce the indies finished albums from submitted master tapes. After these records, cassettes, and C.D.'s have been manufactured, the major then handles distribution of this product using its massive network of branches. This arrangement has many mutual benefits for all concerned. This is beneficial for the indies in that all of these services become centralized . . . beneficial for the majors in that fees are charged the indies for each service provided. By pressing the indies records, the manufacturing facilities of the major are kept operating at capacity which, indeed, helps the profitability of the majors. The same theory applies to distribution. Pressing facilities and distribution are both considered profit centers for the majors, therefore, all business is good. Even though the major and the independent may compete in the marketplace in the areas of promotion and marketing, pressing and distribution are considered separately.

As indicated, there are countless independent record companies and, as the technology necessary to produce and manufacture records continues to become more affordable and accessable to consumers, more independent companies will emerge. There are, however several large independent companies of the industry. Among these are:

(1) **A and M**—A and M Records, based in Hollywood, Ca. was started as a production company by musician Herb Alpert and Jerry Moss in 1962. A and M's holdings include the old Charlie Chaplin movie studios which serve as the company's offices and studios and reportedly one of the best mastering post-production studios on the west coast. This highly successful company was purchased by the Polygram company in 1989 thus changing the nature of this company from independent to major subsidiary.

(2) **Motown Records**—Motown Records, based in Los Angeles, began in Detroit, Michigan by Berry Gordy in 1960. Historically, one of the most successful independent record companies, Motown went through a tremendous period of change in the late 1980's. During the late 1960's well into the 1980's, Motown was known as "The Sound of Young America". During this period Motown was distributed by a number of independent distributors. In the early '80's, this company entered into a distribution deal with the MCA distribution company. Motown ceased to be an independent company in 1988 when it was purchased by MCA records and became an owned and operated part of this major company.

(3) **Island Records**—Island Records, based in New York City, was formed in 1962 by Chris Blackwell and David Betteridge as an outlet for reggae music. This successful company was also purchased by the Polygram Company in 1989.

(4) **Windham Hills Records**—Windham Hills, began in Palo Alto, Ca. in the 1970's and became the premier company for a type of music described as "New Age"—a kind of environmental background music that enjoyed great success in the eighties. Windham Hill, distributed by A and M Records, continues to enjoy great popularity.

From the above descriptions it can be seen that major companies control, virtually, every facet of their destiny by direct ownership, have the financial clout to make things happen and to weather economic crisis. If the majors are and can do all of the above where is the need for the independent company? In comparing the two company types, there are strengths and weaknesses for each.

Historically, the major record companies have been dominant because of the listed strengths, however, because of the sheer size of these organizations they have usually been slow to react to trends in a business whose consumers tend to be trendy. Examples of this were seen in the twenties with the advent of Race records—a name given to music intended for a black audience, in the 1940s after World War II with the explosion of R and B, the advent of Rock and Roll in the fifties, Folk music in the sixties, Disco in the seventies and Rap music in the eighties. With each of these trends the independent record companies were quicker to react and to capitalize. The majors usually followed suit later and where they did, they became dominant. The reverse is usually true during tough economic times: after the Stock Market crash of 1929 the independent companies became virtually extinct; during World War II when the government imposed limitations on the materials used to make records, namely shellac; after the economic crunch of 1979 many indies left the business.

Independent companies are usually willing to take more risks than majors. With the independents small size and relatively small overhead, it can afford to test the waters with less economic trauma than a major. An interesting trend is the concept of major companies funding independent companies, to make them, in effect, the ancillary A and R arm of the major company. Some critics see this as a trend toward more power being given to the majors with the possible effect of making it more difficult for new independent companies to start. As these independent/production companies become the arms of the majors it is feared that they may begin to look less like independent companies and more like new departments within the majors.

Major Record Company Structure

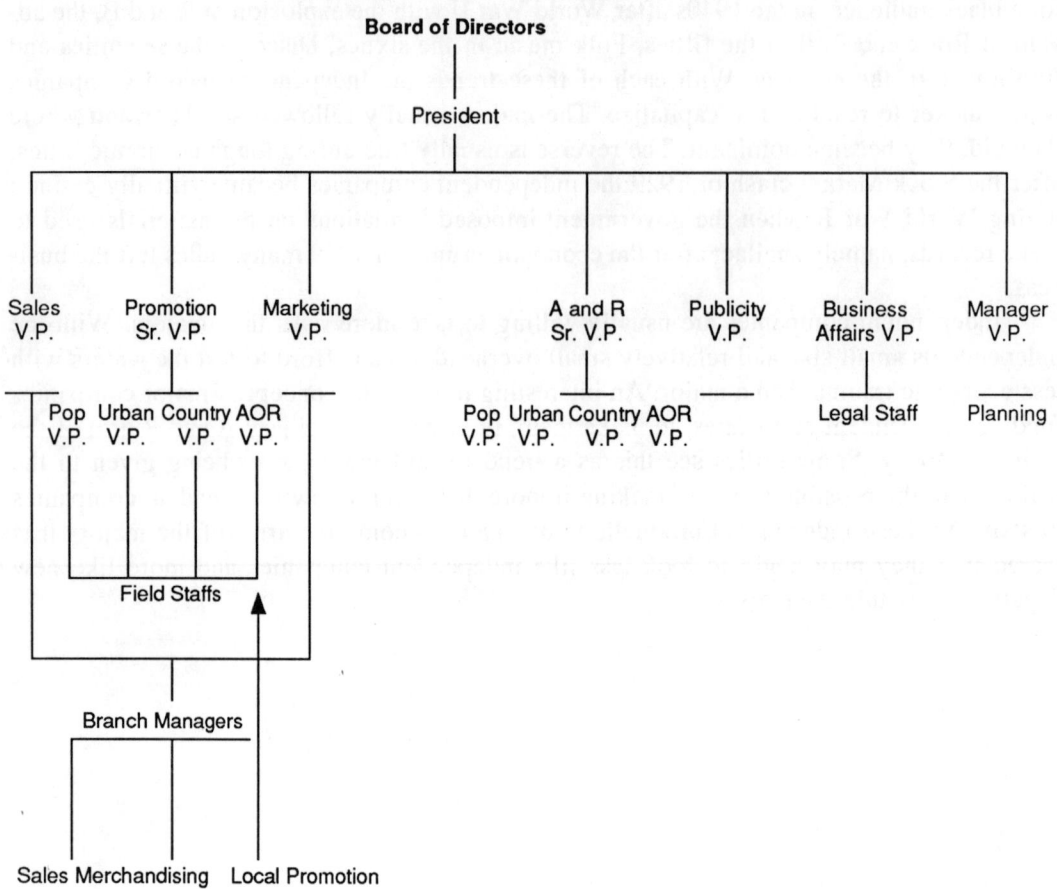

Branch Distribution System

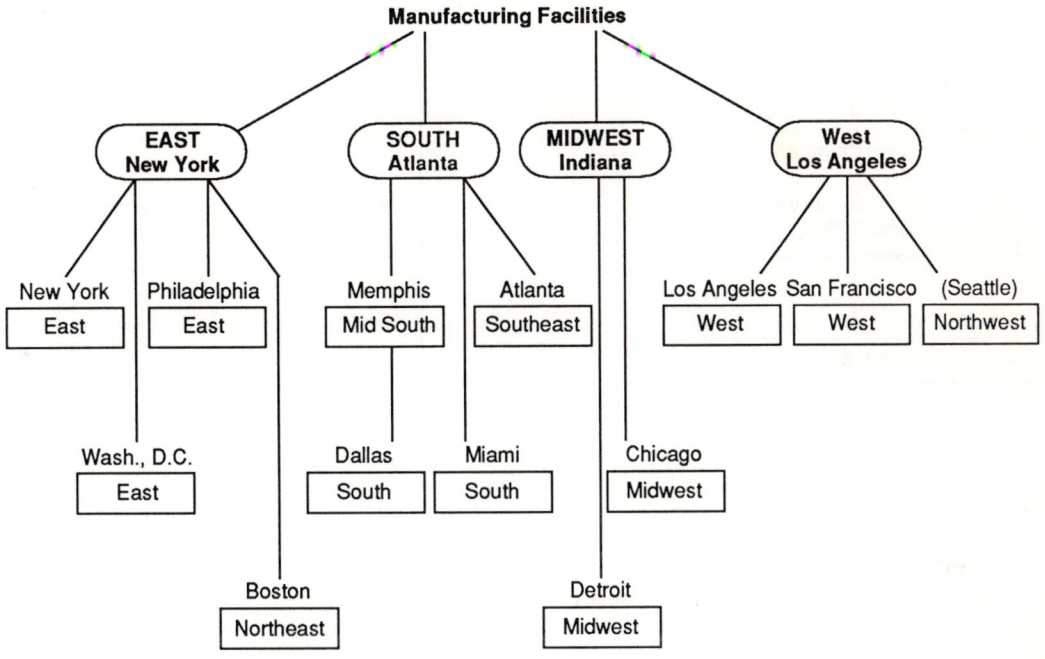

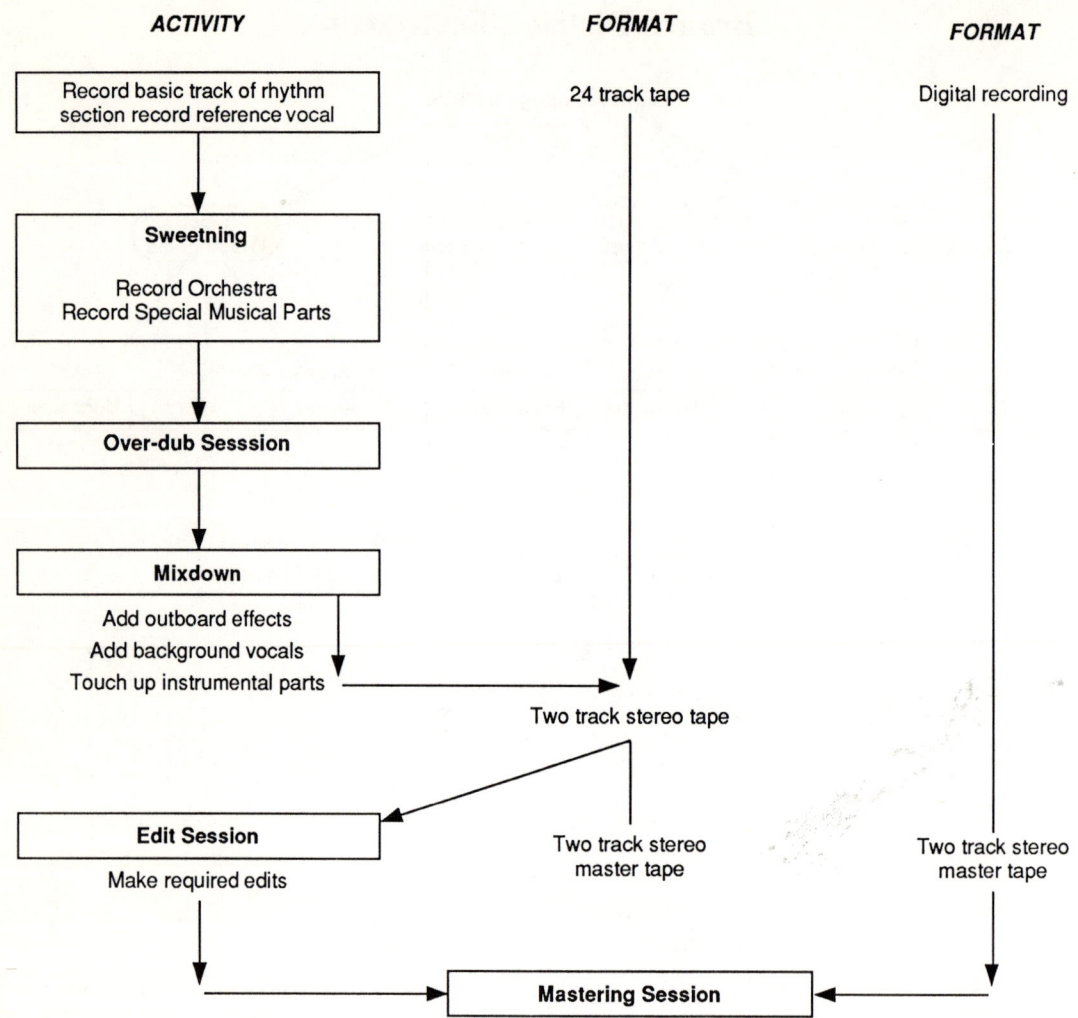

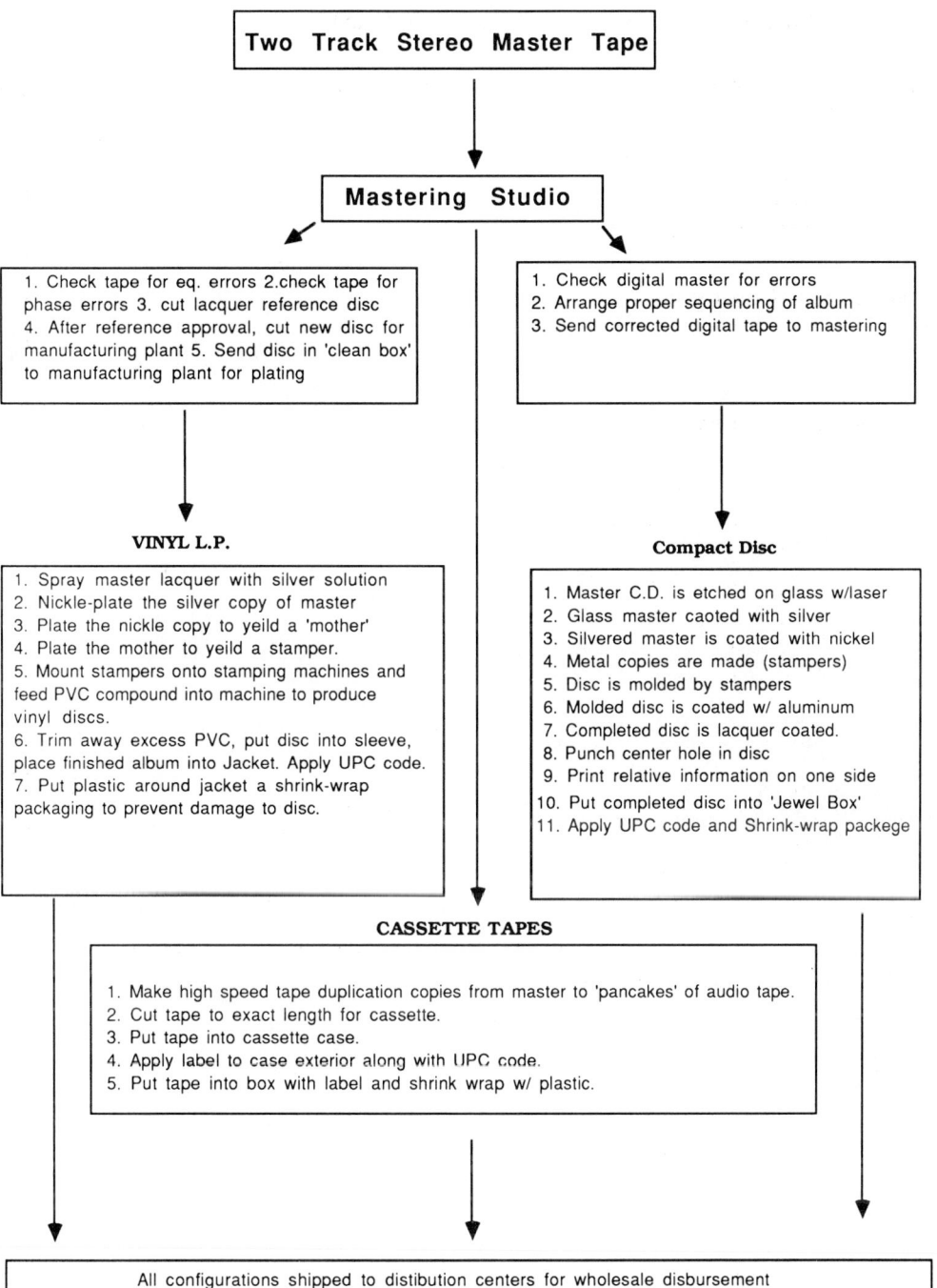

Chapter 4

Placing the Song

Making the Record

Students of the music industry must ultimately ask the question of how the record is actually made. In discussing the mechanism by which a record is produced it is very important to include the various financial propositions required in making the record happen at all.

A record actually begins with an idea and concept—the writing of a song and the performance of it by a group or person which a record company has viewed as having the potential to become very profitable. The company then signs an instrument of commitment—a contract—with the group to make records for which the group will be paid a percentage of the sales of all profitable performances. The actual manufacture of the phonorecord begins in the recording studio with the making of a two track stereo master tape which, in turn, will be reproduced in various configurations and made available for resale. We will examine this process as it applies to the production of an album. The artist, working with a producer, records the material to be included within the album onto a 24 track tape machine. Twenty-four separate audio tracks allow these artists to record the instrumental and vocal tracks individually. The benefit of using a multitrack system in recording is that of giving the artist and producer absolute control in designing and shaping the sound of the various instruments. The first recording done for a song is usually of the rhythm section—drums, guitar, piano, bass. It is from this foundation of instruments the others will be added. When the rhythm track is recorded, many producers use one of the 24 tracks as a reference track. This is done by recording a 'click track'. This track serves as a metronome—a timekeeping device—to insure that proper meter is maintained. There are many producers who do not find the use of this track necessary simply because they believe that highly trained musicians of the rhythm section are such good ones that time is never a problem. However since musicians are human, there is always the possibility of a timing error therefore this timing track proves to be invaluable.

Usually during the recording of the rhythm section a scratch (reference) vocal is also included as part of the session. This vocal is done by the artist and assigned to its own track to serve as a guide to the rhythm section and the producer. This vocal helps the producer as a kind of 'rough draft' of the vocalist's interpretation. This means that it can also be used as a guide for the arranger in deciding exactly how he will place additional instruments in the composition to be recorded at a later date.

After the rhythm section has been recorded, the producer's job is to record the additional instruments if any. If an orchestral arrangement is to be part of this process, it is recorded on the remaining tracks. If background vocals are a part of this performance they are added to the remaining tracks. Usually the last component to be recorded in this rather lengthy process is that of the solo artist's performance. This arrangement of performances is usually done in order to give the solo artist the benefit and necessary advantage of hearing all of the pieces of the compositional puzzle. This can aid in the artist's interpretation of the song.

After the various performances have been recorded they are then combined or "mixed down". The mixing process combines the various instruments and vocal tracks in correct proportion as to provide proper aesthetic proportionality, as the producer sees it, to the composition. He makes sure that the voice is not too loud, music is not too soft, drums are not too overbearing, trumpets are not too loud, violins are heard at the right times, mistakes are removed, and any other myriad combinations that the creators visualize as the proper ingredients for a hit record. The mix down process is extremely important in that an improper mix will usually result in the record not being played, heard, and ultimately sold.

In the 1980's, a new genre of production person became part of the creative musical landscape. This person, the independent re-mixer became especially valuable during the era of disco. This person's specialty was to take a produced master tape and re-mix it in his own image. The theory was that these mixers had a better sense of the dance marketplace than most producers and, indeed, many of the first remix artists themselves were record spinners in night clubs. These new mixes of songs were then marketed by the record companies in the 12 inch record format which could themselves generate a higher resale price than 45 singles. It was also possible for a remix to breathe new life into a record which had been written off as a financial failure by the company. It was also possible to release these 12 inch versions along with the 7 inch single version to provide additional airplay and promotional support to the album, along with providing the company an additional avenue from which to extract profits.

The 12 inch single record market reached its peak during the disco years of the late '70's and early '80's. Even so, this market still remains vital and viable.

The Deal

Record companies operate very much like banks. They follow the same financial planning and cautions that are part of any large business and exercise extreme caution in how corporate assets are expended and are, therefore, very selective about the choices made in spending. Record companies, as any other corporation, has executives: managers charged with generating maximum profits with minimum investment. These managers are accountable and are ultimately, responsible to a board of directors who are in turn responsible to the company's stockholders. This implies a sense of responsibility and prudence.

Although the industry has often been characterized as being carefree and spend thrift, there, indeed, exists a financial framework and procedural protocol for doing business which would rival any other business in the world. A good example of how companies operate can be found in the basic record deal.

Before a record can be produced, several events must occur. First, the act to be recorded must be found. This responsibility, as previously discussed, falls under the domain of the A and R department. A and R's primary concern is to find acts that will fulfill an immediate need—an act which can produce the kind of music that is acceptable and has an appeal for the market the company is trying to reach. This approach is really no different than those used by businesses like auto manufacturers. General Motors, in designing a new sports car, identifies a market which they want to reach. General Motors may do this by conducting extensive marketing research to determine exactly what this market is. The company then designs a car to reach this market, designs an advertising campaign to make this market aware of the car existence, convinces this market that this car is the best of its kind, that the car is available, and tries to show this market that this car will fulfill the market's perceived needs at a cheap price. (Cost/Benefit ratio). In the record business the process is similar yet very different. After an act has been found that the company believes will appeal to a specialized market, a contract must be executed to insure that the company and the act understand what is expected from each party and what the fruits of each party's labor will be. There exists no *standard* contract for an artist but most contracts contain (1) the term of the contract, (2) the number of albums to be recorded under the contract, (3) a maximum amount of money which will be spent for the production of these albums (4) an agreement of exclusivity indicating that the artist is not signed to any other contract and will not sign any other during the term of the contract, (5) a reserve clause indicating how much of an artist's royalty may be withheld to cover contingencies such as the return of unsold records (6) a royalty rate indicating how much an artist will share in the sales of the records, (7) a clause indicating if the contract is territorial or worldwide (8) who chooses songs/material for the album (9) and the right to decide who will produce the album.

Record companies act as banks in that it is the company which has the greater risk: risk in the production and development of acts, the promotion and marketing of a product whose appeal is usually little more than an educated guess, and the risk of appealing to a marketplace which is, at its best, fickle, faddish and unpredictable. All of these activities are expensive and require a significant financial commitment from the companies the least of which for a new act is producing the music. Record companies, in order to protect their interests, make several arrangements within contracts to insure that their investments will pay off. Several of these contractual devices include (1) cross-colateralization of product. Simply stated this means that companies reserve the right to take any deficit from previous albums and apply them to the profits of subsequent albums. This clause allows the company to recoup any production losses. The cost of producing an album is the responsibility of the artist and is paid from artist royalties. This amount is deducted first before any amount is paid to the artist. (2) recoupment clauses against cash advances made on the artist's behalf. Whenever an announcement is made by the trade papers that an artist has been signed to an exclusive deal and that this artist has been given a sizable advance for signing, it is a certainty that, in most cases, this advance is nothing more than that . . . an advance against future royalty payments and will be deducted before any amount is due the artist. The parallel between the company and banks becomes apparent when advances are viewed as interest free loans which have a payback factor inherent in its process.

Companies must also be realistically viewed as corporations who generate their money from the use of income, investments, and loans. Practically speaking, if a company borrows money to support its operations, which include the production of music, and they in turn give artists a cash interest-free advance along with the required funds to produce the music, this is in fact costing the company real dollars in interest points. What the company demands (and gets) for these considerations is the ability to have significant input into how this money is going to be spent.

Companies understand that the relative chances of a record making money are rather slim therefore it reserves the right to retain, at the very least, mutual approval of songs, producers, arrangement of songs on the finished album, album cover design, budgets for studios and musicians, and selection and timing of releases. This simply means that the artist is seldom given free rein in the business aspects of music production and the creative aspect, truly the artist's domain, must fit neatly into prescribed business practices which are in concert with the goals of the company.

Chapter 5

Trade Unions and Associations

The record industry, like many others, is closed in many respects. The industry is, in theory, open to anyone with talent and ability, however movement within the industry is controlled and gauged by a myriad number of trade associations and unions. These unions are responsible, in principal, for insuring that its membership is paid a fair salary for their work, insuring that working conditions are tolerable, for guaranteeing that union personnel will be given priority treatment in securing available work, for guaranteeing which fees and which amount will be paid, and for collecting these fees . . . all of which is guaranteed by the union being recognized as the official collective bargaining agent representing these members. The classical definition for a trade union is that a union secures and enforces minimum standards in working conditions and wages for its membership. As compensation for its role in acting as guardian of worker's rights, the unions are paid fees by its members in the form of membership dues. In addition to membership fees the unions, in some cases, charge a tax on amounts earned by its members. The unions insure their continued participation in negotiating contracts by including within agreements a clause which specifically states that the union will remain the exclusive bargaining agent as long as the members, by majority vote, want this. This has been seen as both good and bad. This proposition has been viewed favorably in that the union cannot be removed unless the workers 'decertify' it and no longer want union representation. Unions do indeed provide a shield between employers and employees. However, in this exclusiveness the unions guarantee membership by requiring that only union members be employed. For many beginning musicians, announcers, and others for whom membership is required, this often presents a financial problem as all unions require an 'initiation' fee before full membership is granted. Another consideration for potential members is in realizing that membership fees are directly proportional to the amount of income generated under the union agreement. This means that there is no set membership fee and that these fees can be very expensive over time. An obvious rationale of the union is that the more income derived from union negotiated contracts, the more the union should realize in income to insure high quality representation for all members, not just those who can afford it.

Whatever the impressions are of industry trade unions, they are going to be around for a very long time.

Industry Performance Trade Unions

The American Federation of Television and Radio Artists

The American Federation of Television and Radio Artists (AFTRA) is responsible for negotiating fees paid to vocalists, both lead and background, on a sound recording and radio/television performing personnel. This can include D.J.'s, news persons, television hosts, persons who speak or are seen in radio and television commercials, and non-news guests for television. AFTRA began as a union to represent radio announcing personnel in 1937. The major mass media performers (and the only ones outside of motion pictures) were the announcers for the national radio networks. As radio evolved into television, AFTRA's jurisdiction was expanded to include its performers. As technology changed the face of mass communication delivery systems, so it changed the face of AFTRA.

It should also be noted that performers in commercials made for television are sometimes required to belong to several unions. If the commercial is recorded on film, the performer must belong to SAG, the Screen Actors' Guild, but if that same commercial is recorded on videotape the performer falls under AFTRA jurisdiction. It is also interesting in that some radio stations which require union membership for its announcers it is required that these announcers be represented a non-announcing union. An example of such an arrangement was that of a San Francisco Bay Area station which, at one time, required its announcers to belong to NABET, the National Association of Broadcast Employees and Technicians, a union whose primary members are engineers. The rationale was that these announcers controlled the station's electronic console in doing their broadcasts therefore they were, essentially, technical personnel.

AFTRA, as a music performance union, represents vocalists, which includes background singers, for all record sessions. AFTRA, through its negotiation with the record industry, has certain minimum requirements for each session. AFTRA requires that all sessions occur only with organizations officially recognized by the union as a 'fair employer'. AFTRA publishes a list through the union's periodical magazine to its membership of unfair producers. These are producers that the union regards as engaging in unfair labor practices such as paying below union scale, using non-union performers, or otherwise not acting in the manner of a fair employer. Any union member who is discovered working for anyone on this list risks suspension or expulsion from AFTRA.

AFTRA's fees for singers on recording sessions are based upon (1) the length of the session, (2) the number of singers that are part of the session, (3) any session which uses three or more singers must also use a *contractor*. This contractor may be the third vocalist but must be paid double scale (2x the minimum session rate) for serving in this capacity.

Fee Structure

AFTRA basis its membership fees on an earned income formula. New members are required to pay an initiation fee of around $300. After this fee is paid, the members are then eligible to participate in the union's pension and welfare fund. Members must earn a minimum amount of money annually to continue as members in good standing. Based on this earned income AFTRA then determines the annual dues for each member. The pension and welfare fund, which supplies benefits such as hospitalization and life insurance to AFTRA members, is funded by employer contributions. AFTRA's pension fund is available to members upon reaching retirement age.

The American Federation of Musicians

The American Federation of Musicians (A.F. of M.) is the union which represents (obviously) musicians, arrangers, orchestrators, and music copyists. The A.F. of M., the oldest U.S. trade union, was formed in the late 1800's to protect the rights of its members who at that time were stage and show musicians. Over the years, A.F. of M. garnered tremendous power via showdowns with the new technologies which, in its opinion, threatened its members guarantees of work. When network radio became a reality in the mid-1920's, the A.F. of M. and its president extracted guarantees from network executives that only union musicians would be hired for these broadcasts. In the motion picture industry, when sound was added to movies in 1926 using the Western Electric Vitaphone system and thus becoming a bigger hit in 1927 with Warner Brother's movie *The Jazz Singer*, the A.F. of M., wanted guarantees of work for its members. Special music written especially for film had been used since the early 1900's which usually required 'house orchestras' as performers. The union's concerns were that this new technology would force the union personnel out of theaters. This issue was resolved when the union was guaranteed union participation in the making of feature film scores. This guarantee also included a fee structure for musicians which would be unique to this new medium. The fees would be assessed not as radio rates but as individual movie rates.

The A.F. of M. responded to radio's use of recorded music by requiring union participation not only in the recording process but, in one instance, the playback of these records. In the 1930's, the Chicago A.F. of M. secured agreements requiring that radio stations hire an A.F. of M. member to control the turntable from which recorded music was played. The union's contention was that a turntable was, in fact, a musical instrument and therefore fell under the A.F. of M.'s jurisdiction. This issue was ultimately resolved by the new technology of audio cassette machines.This new technology meant that radio stations recording the music on tape for playback from a tape machine outside of A.F. of M. jurisdiction.

Fee Structure

For phono-record recording sessions, the A.F. of M., via its national agreements, guarantees minimum fees to be paid to musicians. These fees are based on the union's session rate. A session is defined as being either three (3) hours of work or the recording of two (2) songs. The union also includes within its contracts provisions for each session to include one musician designated as the 'leader'. This musician is paid 'double-scale'— twice the minimum amount for a single musician on a session. Because of the 'leader' requirement, many recording bands/musicians rotate the leader position among themselves so that each may benefit from this contractual provision. The union also requires that a contractor be paid for each session. This person, in theory, is responsible for finding and hiring musicians for each session. The contractor is also paid double scale for providing this service.

In addition to providing its services to musicians, the A.F. of M. also represents copyists and arrangers. The fees charged for these services vary according to the size of the job.

The union derives its income from membership dues and a tax charged each member based upon the amount of work done within its jurisdiction. This tax is deducted from the union members fees which is always paid through the union's office. In order to become a member of the A.F. of M. musicians are required to demonstrate that they are, indeed, musicians. This is done with an audition at the union office. The musician then must pay an initiation fee. The continuing fees are then based on earned income under A.F. of M. jurisdiction. A.F. of M. also assesses a fee to record companies.

Screen Actor's Guild (SAG)

This union's membership includes all performers who appear in films, commercials and any other form which uses film as the medium. SAG is viewed as a very powerful union in economic as well as political terms. Historically, SAG has served as the collective bargaining agent for performers as well as being a very powerful governmental lobbyist. SAG's membership includes many entertainers who also perform recorded music. Because of this SAG has come to have a significant impact upon the record industry. In recent years SAG's influence has grown as the medium of film began to play a major role in the promotion of music with the music industries growing use of produced video clips. Indeed, the most expensive movie made to date, if gauged by the minute, was a music video production to promote the Michael Jackson Thriller album. Many national television outlets such as MTV-Music Television and Video Hits-1, which use film clips as the majority of its programming find themselves or the producers of these 'short movies' negotiating with SAG as these clips fall under this union's jurisdiction. SAG also represents performers who appear in commercials used in television where film was the medium of recording.

Trade Associations

Associations, like unions, are composed of groups of people united under an organizational umbrella to pursue mutual goals. Trade associations, unlike unions, do not engage in collective bargaining or other employment related activities. An association may endorse certain codes of conduct for its membership in seeking to improve the industry and the industry's image but associations do not have the ability to legally force employee/employer relations by making contracts or by using any other union-like method.

The music industry has several associations which exist to foster better communication within its membership and the industry and to increase public awareness of the record industry.

The National Association of Record Merchandisers (NARM)

NARM, which began in the 1950's as an association for a specialized group of music merchandisers known as rack jobbers, has evolved into, arguably, the most powerful association in all of the music business. NARM's regular members are the retail merchants of recorded music who, as a group, represent a very powerful coalition, indeed, for this group will determine a record's ultimate financial success. NARM's associate members include the major record companies as well as most independent manufacturers. It has been said that the center of our solar system may be the Sun but the center of the record industry is most certainly the annual NARM convention as all those responsible for the financial decisions of the industry can be found there.

NARM's activities include formulating policies for enhancing the industry's image and effectiveness. This is accomplished with projects as varied as educating its members about new retail methods to examining the economic impact of piracy and counterfeiting.

The National Academy of Recording Arts and Sciences (NARAS)

NARAS, formed in the late 1950's, is best known for its annual Grammy Awards presentations recognizing excellence in the recording industry. This association's members represent the creative aspect of the music industry. A condition of membership within this association is that the member must have participated and contributed to the production of music that was released commercially and provide evidence of this fact such as album jackets, album labels, or any other part of a release that would indicate this participation. NARM's membership includes singers, writers, producers, arrangers, orchestrators, and musicians.

NARAS's stated purpose is to provide an educational forum for its members and to recognize contributions made to the recording industry. NARAS is financed by annual membership dues and by television revenues generated from its annual awards presentation.

The Black Music Association (BMA)

The BMA was formed in 1978 with its goal being the recognition of the contributions made by Black American music.

The National Association of Television and Radio Artists (NATRA)

NATRA began as an association of Black radio announcers in 1955. The organization grew throughout the 1950's and 1960's and began to include television and recording artists as part of its membership. This organization reached its peak in the mid 70's. During that period NATRA's thrust went beyond music and began to address social issues of the day. NATRA's aim was to provide equal opportunity for all within the entertainment industry. NATRA ceased operations in 1977.

Recording Association of America (RIAA)

The RIAA is the association which represents the views of the record companies. This organization includes within its membership every major record company. There are six major record companies in the United States representing 85% of all records sold. These numbers certainly confirm the power represented by RIAA's membership. RIAA also serves as a clearing house and quasi-accounting firm for the industry. It is from RIAA examination of record company sales figures that Gold and Platinum record awards are determined. By serving as an outside evaluator, the RIAA adds validity and credibility to these awards. Until the mid 70's, Gold and Platinum records were awarded based upon the number of records a manufacturer claimed to have shipped. The RIAA determined that this was not an accurate barometer for determining a record's success since returns—unsold records—could become a part of the count. In order to lessen the possibility of manufactured pseudo-hits, the RIAA required that before a record would be eligible for certification it should have been in the marketplace for at least three (3) months. This amount of time was considered normal for a record to demonstrate weather it was indeed selling and unsold returns were considered.

The RIAA documents and publishes technical standards for the industry and serves as lobbyist in all national and state governmental hearings of concern to the recording industry.

Amusement and Operators Association (AMOA)

The AMOA began in the 1940's as an association devoted to addressing the needs of operators of jukeboxes and, over time, other coin operated entertainment machines. This group also has a tremendous amount of clout within the music industry. Jukeboxes represent a significant financial component of the retail record market.

National Music Publishers Association (NMPA)

This organization was formed in the mid-1900's as an association of writers and publishers. This organization is best known for its ownership of the Harry Fox Agency, its in-house agency responsible for issuing mechanical licenses to the manufacturers of recorded music, for maintaining account information regarding these licenses, and for collection of the generated fees.

National Association of Broadcasters

The NAB, a very powerful lobbyist association, represents the broadcasters of the U.S. It represents, most specifically, owners and managers of broadcast properties. The NAB began in the 1920's as the voice of network radio. It was from the classic confrontation between the NAB and ASCAP that NAB formed Broadcast Music, Inc.

The NAB, based in Washington, D.C., offers many services to its members. Among its various activities are its annual convention, regional workshops, an educational grants program, and a minority clearing house for prospective employers.

Chapter 6

Record Promotion Planning

No matter which format is used by a radio station, record companies have to design a promotion plan around the objectives of these stations. Radio stations are quick to point out that they are not in the business of selling records—they are in the business of selling advertisement. Because of this stark reality, program directors are very conscious and extremely careful of every record they add to a station's play list. Record companies are required to present sound evidence in its attempt to sell the station on the value of its product and, thus, secure an add. This evidence has to include sufficient information to assure the program director that a particular record represents a 'safe' addition to the station list and has the potential of attracting new listeners. Producing and gathering this evidence is accomplished in several ways under the companies *marketing/promotion plan.*

Upon release of a record, the record company—through its promotion department—immediately attempts to identify which formats are likely to find this release appealing. These designated stations are then targeted for initial airplay and given priority as those stations which the promotion field staff *must* deliver by securing favorable airplay. If the record is by a new artist, these targeted stations are usually found in the smaller *secondary* and *tertiary* radio markets. These 'small market' stations are approached first because it is assumed that these program directors are more likely to take the risk of playing an unfamiliar artist. The logic which explains this willingness to test an untried artist is that in smaller markets, the competition from other music format stations is far less intense than in the major markets.

In the major markets with a population of 500,000+, each unfamiliar record played by a station represents a possible *tune-out factor* for its audience . . . that is, an invitation to its listeners to punch the button or turn the dial to another station that *is* playing familiar music. Each listener a station manages to lose represents a potential additional listener for the station's competition. If a program director makes enough mistakes or misjudgments about the musical tastes of his/her audience and unwittingly drives enough listeners *away* from the station, the next activity may well be the program director being driven away. The program director, in selecting bad music or music not right for his format, has now, in fact, become a station liability.

Since radio stations are businesses and, as such, motivated by profit margins and since loss of listeners equals loss of revenue, loss of listeners usually also represents loss of a job for the program director. This real fear of program directors—the possibility of losing more than ratings—and their real reluctance to add new records by new artists, makes the record promotion person's burden to produce sound evidence of a record's viability paramount.

The next step in the promotion plan involves several inter-related activities which must be executed with precision and timing. The promotion department must make sure that the stations adding the release report this fact to the trade magazines. It is from these station reports that the trades generate chart position and assign numbers to records. If the promotion department convinces enough stations to add the record, the record will show up on the charts with a *bullet*. A bullet is the chart's visual representation around the record's number to indicate that this record is moving up the chart and should be watched carefully. As soon as the record is added in the target market, the record company sales department must make sure that enough records are in the stores of each targeted area to supply the (hopeful) demand once airplay begins. The sales department also asks music retailers to report sales activity to the trades and to the local station playing the record. The local station usually considers the factors of (1) local sales, (2) national chart position and (3) audience requests when deciding weather a record moves up, down or off the station chart. As the record moves up the chart, its rotation (amount of airplay received) increases. As the amount of radio airplay increases for a record, its chart position is improved in the national ratings of industry trade magazines. So it can be seen that this relationship is symbiotic and semi-perpetual as, these elements feed each other. As soon as either side in the equation changes its position, the other side reacts to reflect the new status of a record.

Once the record is on the charts and being played in heavy rotation in these markets, the promotion department then takes this evidence—the chart positions, the list of stations playing the record, and the rotation—to the secondary market stations. The entire process repeats itself until the record is placed in major markets.

Once the record is receiving across-the-board play it then becomes the record company's top priority to maintain chart position for as long as possible. Generally, as long as a record stays on the top position of the charts, the record will continue to receive exposure. As the record nears the end of its initial life cycle, usually between 12 and 16 weeks, the record company will attempt to keep the record on the charts until another release is ready to be sent out and the process started over again. For the second release, however, the job will be a little easier because the new act now has name recognition and programmers usually assume that an artist who did well before will surely do well again. Even though this is not always the case, stations will usually give the act the benefit of the doubt and consider them a smaller risk factor.

The process of adding a release of a major act is entirely different. When a major act, known for having wide audience appeal, releases a new record, programmers are targeted across the country. The major markets are usually given priority with many gimmicks such as 'world exclusives' and these releases are usually supported by heavy advertising commitments using radio as the primary vehicle.

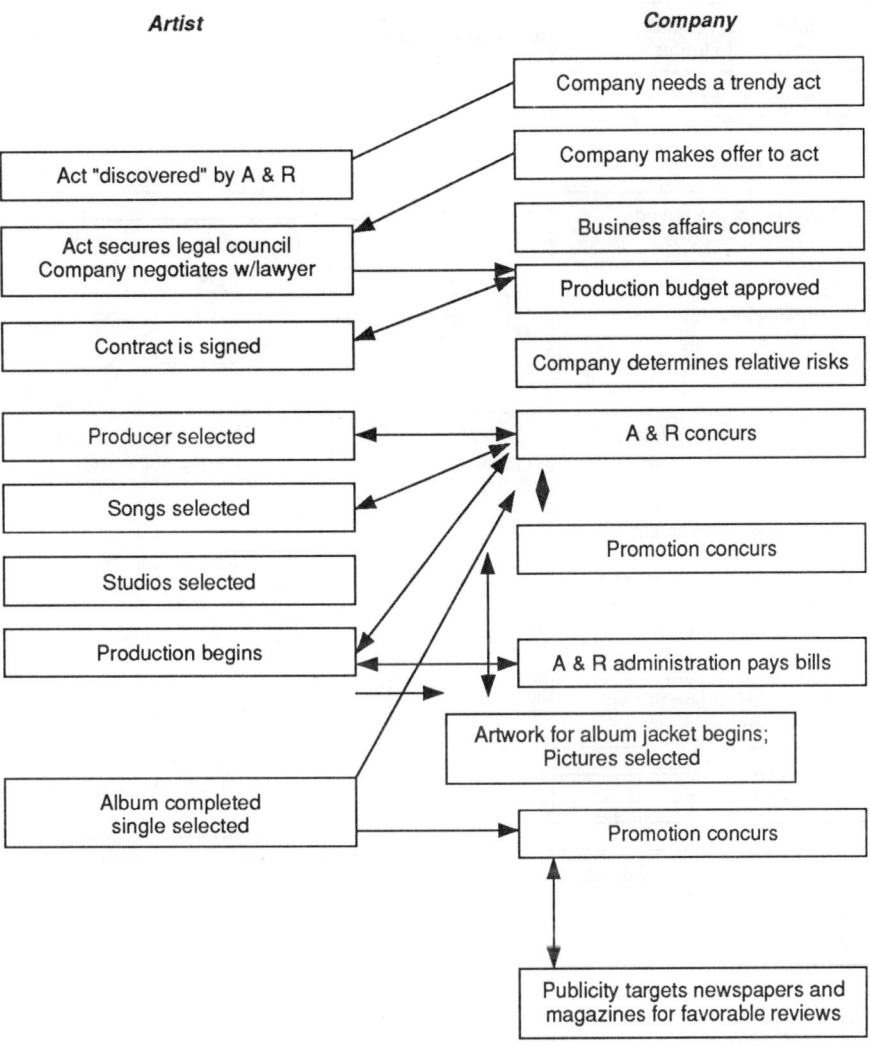

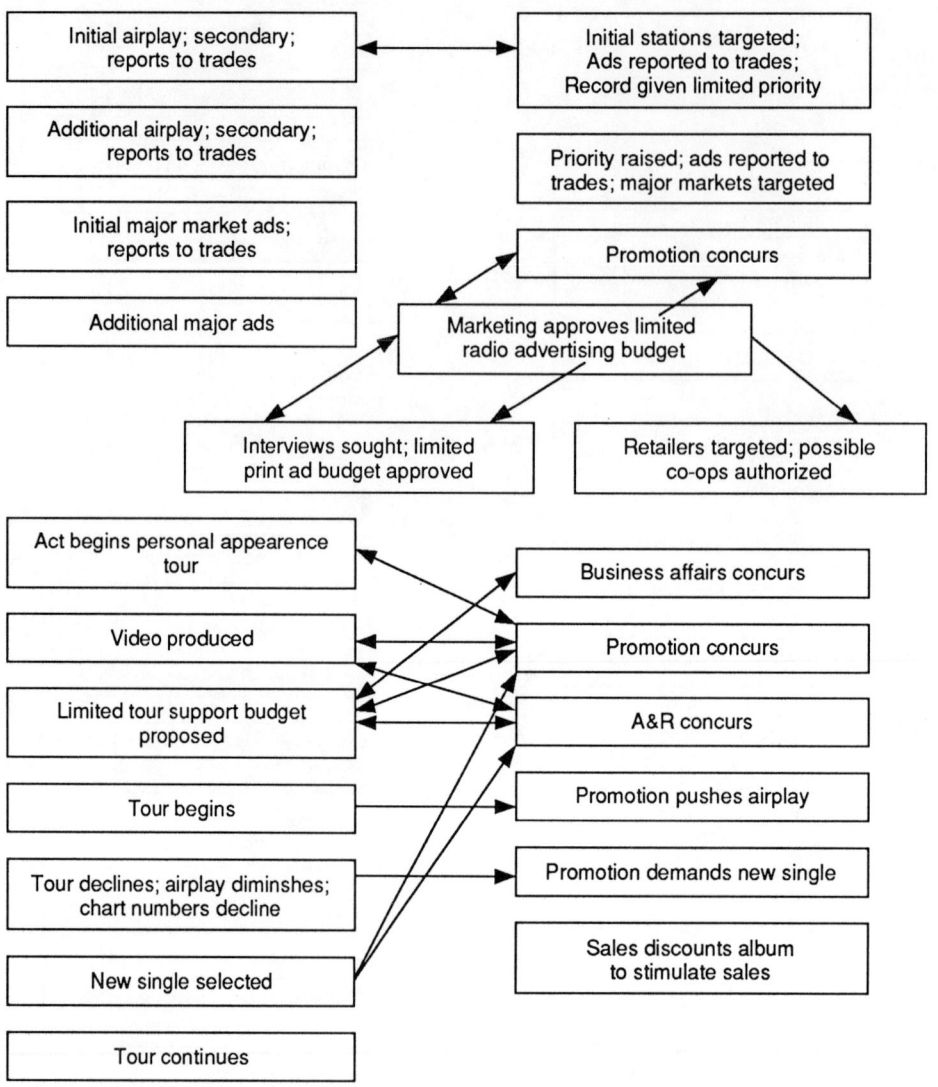

Record Life Cycles

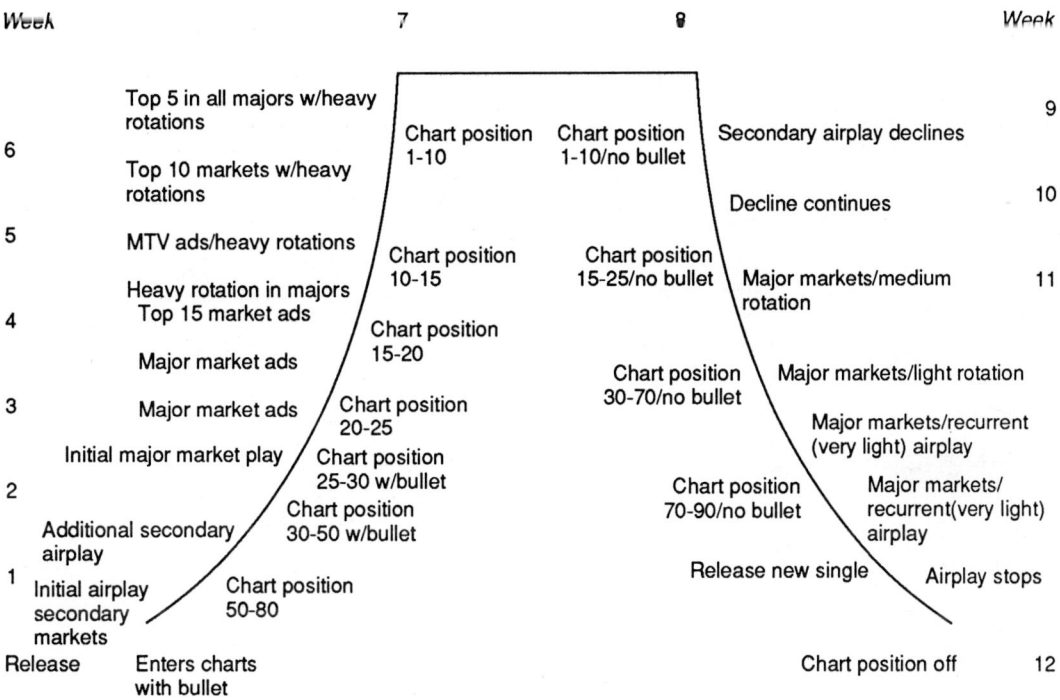

Chapter 7

Charts

No other indicators of the record industry cause as much anxiety or exhilaration as the record charts. Charts, those harbingers of mixed tidings to the participants of the business, are the weekly record surveys. These surveys are published weekly by the industry's leading trade magazines. These reports indicate which records are active and how this activity is to be interpreted. The dynamics of the charts are always based on *relative* performance. This means that a record's chart position must always be evaluated by also examining the performance of every other record on that week's survey. An example of how this might work can be seen in examining records that have been charted as number one (#1). Since the number one record is deemed the most popular record of that week, it could be assumed that the number one record is also a great seller. This is not always the case. If the entire industry is in the middle of a slow sales period, all records are affected. This then means that a number one record, considered a hit by the chart listing standard, may not be a great selling record even though it performed better during the sample week than other records on the chart and, when compared to them, was indeed number one. Charts represent, at their best, the relative performance of the listed records and, at their worst, the survey response of a record's potential to become a success.

Charts are *extremely* important when it is seen that a record's chart position affects so many aspects of the record's destiny. Contained within this destiny are the fates and fortunes of the artist, the producer, the artist's manager, the profitability of the record company, the activity of booking agents, and every other person or organization who profits from a record's success. The charts additionally serve as indicators to radio stations and have a tremendous influence in aiding them with music programming decisions.

Radio, still the number one promotion vehicle for records, watches a record's progress (or lack of it) via the charts and, subsequently, uses this information in determining which records are worthy of continued airplay, greater airplay, or deserving to be eliminated from the station playlist. Since exposure by radio airplay translates (ideally) into sales and since this exposure is controlled—to a degree—by the charts, the industry's need to make an impressive chart showing is, to say the least, motivated. Charts are used by record retailers in much the same way that stock market listings are used by brokers and buyers. Retailers use the charts in determining which records should be ordered in a greater supply, which ones probably are a bad buy and should be returned, and which artists should be watched as potential large volume artists. Booking agents use the charts to help determine which acts should be considered for concert dates, what the act's billing should be, and how much money would be acceptable for a live concert date. Charts are a significant indicator of an artist's popularity and bankability. Within the record company, charts are used in formulating a number of policy and creative decisions including when an artist's record should be released and when it should be withdrawn; they are used to verify an artist's track record when an artist is trying to negotiate a new deal with a company. Companies use charts, along with sales figures, to gauge every aspect of a record's performance and are further used in evaluating departmental performance, especially promotion, and in gauging personnel effectiveness. Other company decisions made around chart information include those regarding a company's market positioning, and company image.

Charts, in a word, are everything to the industry. When considering the charts, it should be noted that the system employed in their assembly is not fail-safe . . . they are much akin to television and radio audience ratings systems in that they are only *estimates* but, still, they are viewed by the industry as vital and continue to exert an enormous amount of influence.

Record charts have been around, virtually, as long as there has been a record industry. The earliest chart was *John Peatman's Record Survey* published in the U.K. during the 1920's. American music charts came into existence during the late 1920's with Billboard magazine's listing of those songs being heard on network radio. As the years progressed and the industry grew and became more diverse, the charts grew. The most influential charts today include those published by Billboard magazine. Billboard, published weekly, contains a number of charts, each reflecting the relative popularity of music in specialized segments. The Top 100 in Billboard represents those records with the greatest activity within the industry defined area of Pop (popular, mass appeal) music. Other charts published weekly within Billboard include those for Urban Contemporary (Black Music), Country, Jazz, Gospel, New Age, Album Oriented Rock, Dance (club activity) and a supplement of charts from countries around the world.

Other important charts include those found within other industry publications which include Cashbox magazine, Radio and Records, The Gavin Report, and HITS magazines. Within each magazine are charts which represent, like Billboard, the activity of records within various categories.

As previously indicated, these charts are considered the barometers which indicate a record's relative popularity. Relative popularity simply indicates that it is possible for a record in an economically depressed marketplace to occupy a high position on a chart and, yet, remain unprofitable. Chart position is determined by many factors including each record's performance as measured against the performance of other charted records. The methodology employed in determining this popularity is by survey. Each trade magazine conducts a weekly telephone survey of radio stations and retail record outlets. Because it is highly impractical for the magazines to call every record store and radio station in the country, the magazines use a representative sampling as the basis for its surveys. The progress of a record is monitored to examine how it is selling and playing against other records in several marketplaces. The radio station aspect of the survey is conducted by questioning a cross-section of stations in key markets that have been assigned a 'point value' by the magazine. A station's worth is determined by the size of the market the station serves, the popularity of the station, as evidenced by rating reports, and the stations historical significance as a 'bell-weather'' in predicting or substantiating hits. All of these factors are watched very closely by record companies as they indicate the value of an addition to a particular station's playlist. This information is then used by record companies in establishing promotion strategies and priorities. The companies, logically, reason that a station worth 10 points is certainly worth more allocated promotion man-power and time than a station worth 2 points.

By discovering which records have been added or deleted from a radio station's weekly list of hits or which records have moved up or down in rotation (frequency of play), and by getting other indications of key activities which support a record—such as telephone requests from station listeners—promotion experts can gauge which aspects of the promotion campaign need to be refined or abandoned.

Radio programmers have similar, yet, different concerns regarding chart positions. One of the programmer's main concerns is to determine how a record should be dayparted. Music programming is concerned not only with how often a record is played (rotation) but which time of the day this play occurs (dayparting). This concern of programmers is, by definition, a concern of record companies who want to make sure that as many ears as possible are exposed to their product. The difference is that programmers are concerned with quality—if the record is really a hit—while record companies are concerned with quantity—how many listeners will this record reach. Another way to state how these two diverse yet symbiotic needs are seen is the radio stations are concerned as to if a record will attract additional listeners to the station without driving those already tuned to the station away. Record companies, on the other hand, are concerned with a record being exposed to the largest possible audience in the hopes that this exposure will translate into sales. Both are selling—radio is selling station image, record companies are selling records—yet not for or to each other.

To better understand how dayparting works, a very minimal understanding of radio programming is required. The twenty-four (24) hour broadcast day is divided into various segments by the major audience research companies. These segments are named and, in theory, correspond to accurate descriptions of the audience available to listen to radio at these times. These periods are: 6:00–10:00 A.M. (morning drive); 10:00–2:00 P.M. (midday); 2:00–6:00 P.M. (afternoon drive); 6:00 P.M.–12:00 A.M. (evenings) and 12:00 A.M.–6:00 A.M. (overnight). The most important times to obtain radio airplay are in the respective drive periods; morning and afternoon. Morning drive is considered the most valuable of time at a radio station and thus, for a record to be exposed. It is during this period that most listening occurs and most audience is available. Stations charge their highest prices for advertisements broadcast during this period because of this large, captive (usually in cars and on their way to work), and available number of ears tuned to various radio stations.

Programmers want to be sure that any record played during this period will not result in the loss of a single listener. Records within the Top 20 chart positions are usually played more during this period than any other. The theory suggests to programmers that these top 20 records represent the 20 most popular records and therefore are the safest to play.

The next most valuable time is the afternoon drive period. Again, programmers will usually stick with the proven hits. In the mid-day period the audience is assumed to be older, therefore, programmers will change the mix of music to reflect this audience, usually by adding a wider variety of music including re-currents, records not quite old enough to be considered 'oldies' yet not current enough to be considered 'demand' hits. The evening period is assumed to be a much younger audience—primarily teenagers—therefore a less mature artist would do well in this period. Most programming experimentation occurs in the overnight period when the station has the least amount to lose—listeners and advertising revenues.

Record stores are polled by chart assemblers to check the movement and actual sales or records. These stores, as the final link in the chain from manufacturer to consumer, are considered to be the most accurate source to check for a record's sell through—the actual hard sales of titles. These sales reports are very important, especially for album chart numbers. It is not uncommon for the record buyer of a large record store or chain of stores to be lobbied by record companies. These buyers take on the trappings of importance of radio programmers and are very important to record companies in that these labels want the buyer to remember them when the trades call for a report of a record's progress. The record buyer is also important for local surveys, those conducted by local radio stations to determine the relative movement of records in that local market.

In determining how far a record moves up the charts, the trades consider a mix of information supplied by the retailer. For single records, chart positioning, the dominant factor is radio acceptance and amount of airplay given a record. . . . Additions to playlists and rotation reports are considered the barometers for singles until these records reach about the halfway mark (50) up the chart. From the mid-point to the top, the charts consider a combination of airplay, sales, rotation, and movement of other records in relationship to the single.

For albums, the primary consideration is sales information. The album chart is much less volatile then the singles chart. The life of an album is, typically (and, hopefully) much longer than that of a single, therefore, it seems logical that the progress of an album would be gauged by cumulative sales figures.

Record companies usually provide the charts with general sales information in order to aid in obtaining a favorable report and listing. Along with this information, companies engage in very aggressive print advertising campaigns via the trade magazines. These ads, not intended for the general public, generate interest from the retailers, radio, agents, and every other entity that has an interest in viewing the company's commitment to an act.

As a record moves up the charts, it is given 'indicators' to show those evaluating a record weekly activity. Those indicators include columns indicating how long a record has been on the charts, its position this week and a 'bullet'. The bullet, a circle around the number of the record indicates that this record is a mover and should be watched. Bullets indicate, in theory, that the record is very active and will continue to go up on the charts. When a record loses its bullet, companies use this information to determine whether a new release is in order, do promotion strategies need adjusting, or if sales figures correspond with chart position. A record which has been on the charts for 3 weeks, is in the #50 position with no bullet after having been at #30 with a bullet for 1 week, will most certainly be viewed as a record with very little potential for continued growth.

The charts are not perfect or infallible but they are a major information component in the music promotion, merchandising sales, and radio programming system. Reading charts accurately is a skill, which when developed, resembles how a stock broker reads the financial market. Charts are very helpful as far as giving companies tangible feedback in devising and adjusting marketing strategies.

Critics of the chart system say the methodology used in assembling chart information is flawed in that they are assembled using unverifiable and subjective opinions from reporters and that too many 'vested interests' can be served by giving less than accurate reports. Whatever the arguments, the charts will remain the central barometer of the industry for the near future.

Chapter 8

Radio

The radio industry is often mistaken as being a part of the record industry but is a tremendous industry within itself. Radio is, in many ways, the vehicle which carries the music industry down its road to success. Radio is all important in the promotion of recorded music as most exposure of new product is accomplished by radio air play. Radio is often described as being a companion medium . . . the radio listener is usually doing other things while listening but it is still clear that the music is heard. Given the vital importance of radio exposure in the general marketing of recorded music, it is very important that the record company promotion executive understand as much as possible about how radio stations operate. The record promotion person has to develop the ability to understand and find ways of obtaining exposure for his company's records in much the same manner that the publishing company song pluggers of the early 20th century had to find ways to convince entertainers to use their material in live shows. Understanding programming techniques will indeed aid the promotion person obtain exposure. Radio with its unique ability to reach specialized markets, has tremendous influence and, therefore, tremendous power in the recorded music industry.

Radio reaches its audiences by way of formats. These formats are organized game plans that dictate which records will be played, how many records will be played, how often records will be played, the style of announcers used to present the music, and determine the content of everything else between the music. These varied formats are designed to reach a very specific part of the general radio listening audience. Radio programmers, since the early fifties, have recognized that a station is much more successful if its programming scheme targets specific listeners rather than try to be all things to all people. This specific audience represents a demographic slice of the population pie and, as such, is identified by gender, age, race, and earning/spending potential and patterns.

From the 1920's (the beginning of radio programing) until the 1940's (considered to be the 'Golden Age' of radio), *network*s primarily determined programming content and trends. Music programming was fairly simple when compared to the elaborate research methods employed in contemporary programming techniques. The networks supplied programming which consisted of a mixture of soap operas, comedy shows, quiz shows and musical variety shows featuring live bands and their featured singers. Radio had become, more or less, vaudeville removed from the live theater and transplanted lock, stock, and corney jokes to this electronic medium. As far as network executives were concerned, intellectual content was irrelevant . . . this formula made money. This certainly does not imply that today's programmers have taken a different view of programming content for the profit margin still dictates program decisions. Rather, network radio set the pattern and practices which still exist today. The network formula worked rather well for almost thirty years until the advent of another new technology—television.

Television had, technically, been on the horizon as long as radio. Its development had been delayed by many factors including the Stock Market crash of 1929, and World War II. With the end of the war in 1945, the networks proceeded full speed ahead with the development of national television services.

With the introduction of network television to the American public in the late '40's, many of the entertainers responsible for generating the programs of network radio deserted it to become part of this great new medium. As this happened, along with the American public becoming more aware each day of this new medium, consumers purchased more televisions. Thus, as more viewers became available to watch television, the television networks began to supply more network television programming to meet this demand. As the torrid love affair between television and the American public grew, the impact of radio diminished. This meant that the available audience for radio suddenly and dramatically was no longer available. The effect of less audience translated to vastly reduced advertising profits for the network and its affiliated stations. In order for the local affiliate stations, which had depended on the networks for programming and revenues, to survive, these stations had to discover innovative methods of reaching what was left of their old audiences and to cultivate new legions of listeners.

Audience size has always been of paramount importance to radio given the function that how many listeners a station has determines how much revenue that station will generate from advertising sales. With the financial survival of local radio at stake, a programming alternative had to be developed. This development was realized with the introduction of *format radio*.

In the beginning, this new station presentation to the public was considered, indeed, innovative in that instead of live bands, the music came from records. Instead of program announcers with deep, resonant tones introducing the featured singers and commercials, the announcers introduced and played pre-recorded music. These announcements consisted of introductions of recorded performers and of reading commercials but were also geared toward the local community in which the station was located. These *'disc jockeys'* and the recorded music they played became the key to reaching a local audience by tailoring programming to create the illusion of the local station belonging to the local community. The kind of music presented also helped in reaching and developing the "new" audience, in this case—teenagers. The most important factor in considering this audience of 'kids' was financial. . . . These new consumers had money and represented tremendous buying power. The music formula used to reach this audience evolved from a system adapted from network radio and, most recently, network television. 'Your Hit Parade', a weekly network program had become very successful by using the formula of playing the most popular songs every week. This popularity was determined by conducting surveys of record sales and by examining the trade magazine charts. These charts were the result of trade surveys of record stores and record companies. The assembled charts, therefore, were measures of a record's relative popularity.

The networks had also discovered that a very wealthy market existed in the 18–24 year old age group with whom Your Hit Parade was number one. The two radio pioneers given credit for understanding how this formula could be translated and transferred to local radio programing are Tod Storz and Gordon McLendon. As with most innovations in entertainment, there are different historical versions of who *really* did propose format radio programming but, it is without dispute that Storz and McLendon introduced a system for programming radio which did, indeed, revolutionize broadcasting concepts.

In examining this new philosophy it was clear that foremost in program design was uniformity in the sound of the station. Storz and McLendon's basic formula was to simply (1) limit the number of records played by the station to 40 records. This was unheard of in the early fifties as announcers who played records were allowed to bring and play their individual selections to work therefore each had a different sound to reach what each announcer perceived as their individual audience however these initial programmers understood that for a station to succeed it must have a uniform sound. Storz and McLendon also understood that familiarity was key. Every record played with great regularity had to be familiar to the audience and they must be heard often.

These *Top 40* records would be selected from national record listings and would be the 40 most popular. In addition to the limited list, announcers would be required to play the records in a set pattern. The top ten records, would be given the greatest exposure, the next ten a little less and so on throughout the list. The ideas was that the more popular a song, the more the audience would want to hear it. This formula for record play coupled with very heavy promotion of the station's activities, lots of contests, record hops, and high energy announcers brought immediate success to local radio.

As the years passed and radio markets developed, radio programming became more competitive. As more stations turned to recorded music as the key format element, competition became fierce to reach the target audience. The key for success became not only how well you played music but how well you defined and reached the designated target audience. Audiences became more sophisticated radio listeners and stations responded by designing formats to reach not only audience segments, but segments within segments. In the 1950's, Top 40 radio reached primarily teenagers; R and B radio reached primarily a Black audience. Programmers discovered that audiences were transient and were not wholly dedicated to any one station. As social conditions changed within the country and the audience segmented further, this elusive core audience became much more difficult to pin down. Then, with the popularization of F.M. radio in the late 1960's, audiences segmented even more as new formats emerged. Station programming philosophies began to resemble war strategies, complete with 'objectives maps' and organizational flow charts as part of the process. Stations began using hot clocks—visual representations of how the broadcast elements should be tied together—and unyielding program structure became the order of the day.

Within each decade since the introduction of format radio there have been enormous changes in how music is presented. As simply "living" gave way to "lifestyles", radio had to adjust to reflect the habits, likes, and dislikes of its target audiences and had to do it with the precision of a surgeon for as these years passed, the competition became fiercer from other station competing to reach the same audience.

The dominant formats used in American broadcasting today include CHR, AOR, Country, Urban Contemporary, Adult Contemporary, and other less important formats for the promotion of contemporary music such as classical, news/talk, foreign language, and educational.

Within each of the music formats lies a system which the record companies must understand in order to persuade the gatekeepers—those persons responsible for the selection and placement of music within the station play list, in this case the program and music directors—to include its product as part of the station's playlist and rotation. The *rotation*, how often a record is played and how many times throughout the entire broadcast day a record is exposed, is all important. The frequency of a record being played (how the record is placed within rotation) and heard (a function of audience size) determines how many consumers are exposed to the record. This becomes vital in that the first place a consumer usually hears a new record is via radio. To understand how this is done we should first describe the various formats.

Contemporary Hit Radio

The CHR format is really an updated version of the Top 40 format of the fifties and sixties. This format is recognized by a play list which, in the purest incarnation of this format, is taken directly from the top 30–50 records of the national trade magazines. The announcers for these stations are usually young with a rapid fire delivery. The Top Ten records receive the greatest amount of play with a sprinkling through the day of recurrents—records not quite old enough to be considered oldies and no longer new enough to be considered 'new'. This format uses very little news, except in the morning shows.

Urban Contemporary

This format is the latest incarnation of the old R and B presentation. Urban Contemporary is, according to several of its program directors, not really an updated rhythm and Blues format which was intended to reach primarily a black audience, but more the logical extension of a seventies format, Disco, and designed to reach a wide audience spectrum. The disco format was a high energy, dance oriented, presentation designed to reach a young audience. This highly successful format achieved prominence by playing a wide range of music, usually up tempo, and selecting music based more on beat than lyrics and to include this range of music regardless of perceived racial appeal. In the eighties the Urban Contemporary format had tremendous success in many of the nation's major markets. In New York City (WRKS), Chicago (WGCI), Detroit (WJLB), Washington,

D.C. (WKYS), San Francisco (KSOL) this became the dominant format. It has been suggested that the success of this format has, in many ways, changed the face of the CHR format in its selection and inclusion of black music as part of its rotation and listing. The U/C format's greatest appeal is to a predominantly black audience.

Country

The country format is identified by a play list which contains the current country stars. The listing of importance of these records is determined by trade magazine listings. This format in the eighties saw a division and distinction between two expressions of country. Urban country became the format which featured top country stars with more of a soft approach to the music. Many of the songs played in this format are lush productions with large orchestras. In the traditional county format many of the songs are orchestrated using instruments that identify with the US country sound like the steel guitar. Each expression of this format is intended to reach a specific audience. The Urban country format, as its name implies, is geared to the up scale city fan—a la Urban Cowboy—while the traditional country format is intended for the most dedicated of country listeners.

AOR

The AOR format consists of a play list which features, mostly, album selections. This format usually uses a very casual approach to the presentation of its music. The announcers are usually very low key with the music featured as the star. The music list is assembled using national charts and by selecting album tracks from artists who have had a strong appeal to this format's target audience. The AOR format is intended to reach a young market, however the 1980's saw a division within this format. One expression of the 80's AOR format is designed to reach the so called 'baby boom' generation, these listeners between the ages of 30–45, many of whom listened to Underground Radio, the predecessor of AOR. Underground was a format of the 60's and early '70's that represented itself as being the voice of the various youth counter-culture movements.

A recent AOR format expression features, logically, records from the sixties and seventies as part of its rotation. The more modern expression of the 80's AOR format presentation featured only the latest rock albums within its rotation.

Adult Contemporary

The most widely used format in contemporary radio is simply called Adult Contemporary. To define this format depends very heavily upon whom you ask, however, there is no question which audience segment is the target of these stations. The A/C format is identified by a musical mix of very popular artists who have been determined to reach an audience between the ages of 35–49. This audience represents a very powerful economic segment and is therefore highly desirable to advertisers. The announcers within this format are usually of a moderate energy sound. The information presented is topical and current and the overall station sound is less 'intense' than other contemporary music formats.

De Facto Networks

The 1980's saw an interesting development in local radio programming that had a strong resemblance to radio of the 1920's. With the advent of satellite technology and its availability to the general public, radio saw the formation of new radio networks. This new system of program delivery via satellite gave many entrepreneurs the opportunity to reach specialized audiences by providing specialized programs to local stations. Among the most successful of these networks is Westwood One based in Los Angeles. By bartering program time to the nation's stations appealing to a young audience, this company managed to produce enough in profits to purchase the Mutual Broadcasting System, an old line radio network. Later Westwood One purchased much of the old NBC Radio operation. This highly successful company managed this herculean feat by packaging programs, offering them to broadcasters without charging fees in exchange for a certain varying number of commercial minutes from the client station. By then selling this time to advertisers for an audience created by Westwood One, this company enjoyed healthy profits by putting an interesting twist upon an old idea: by providing non-exclusive network programming to stations who would become, in effect, partners in a time/barter system very similar to network television.

Other companies have used this same formula and become program suppliers—a little less than a full-blown network but providing programs to stations under, usually a barter arrangement.

Program Suppliers*

ABC Contemporary Radio Network
125 West End Ave.
New York, NY 10023
(212) 887-5441
FAX: (212) 887-5314

ABC Direction Radio Network
125 West End Ave.
New York, NY 10023
(212) 877-5192
FAX: (212) 887-5533

ABC Entertainment Programming
ABC Watermark
125 West End Ave.
New York, NY 10023
(212) 887-5365
FAX: (212) 887-5449

ABC Entertainment Radio Network
125 West End Ave.
New York, NY 10023
(212) 887-5553
FAX: (212) 887-5533

ABC FM Radio Network
125 West End Ave.
New York, NY 10023
(212) 887-5635
FAX: (212) 887-5314

ABC Information Radio Network
125 West End Ave.
New York, NY 10023
(212) 887-5585

ABC Radio Networks
125 West End Ave. 7th Fl.
New York, NY 10023
(212) 887-5200
FAX: (212) 887-5533, (212) 887-5534

ABC Rock Radio Network
125 West End Ave.
New York, NY 10023
(212) 887-5652
FAX: (212) 887-5533

ABC Talkradio
125 West End Ave.
New York, NY 10023
(212) 887-5638
FAX: (212) 887-5533

About Radio Enterprises
4820 Coldwater Canyon Ave, Ste. 106
Sherman Oaks, CA 91423
(818) 377-4300

Airlines
20028 Woodmont
Harper Wods, MI 48225
(313) 881-4551

Airways
P.O. Box 1075
Champaign, IL 61820
(217) 359-6782

AKG Acoustics, Inc.
77 Selleck St.
Stamford, CT 06902
(203) 348-2121
FAX: (203) 324-1942

All Media
305 N. Harbor, Ste. 315
Fullerton, CA 92632
(714) 879-9153
FAX: (714) 871-6710

All Star Radio
3575 Cahuenga Blvd. W., Ste. 255
Los Angeles, CA 90068
(213) 850-1169
FAX: (213) 850-1610

*Excerpted From pages 67-82 of the *R & R DIRECTORY* VOL. 1 '89.

The Aloha Radio Network
"Country Plus"
1750 Kalakaua Ave, Ste. 3–229
Honolulu, HI 96826
(800) 248–7587
FAX: (808) 526–1537

Alternative Programming, Inc.
2501 Oak Lawn, Ste. 365
Dallas, TX 75219
(800) 231–2818, (214) 521–4484
FAX: (214) 521–6808

American Comedy Network
Park City Plaza
10 Middle St.
Bridgeport, CT 06604–4277
(203) 384–9443
FAX: (203) 367–9346

American Image Productions
1719 West End Avenue, Ste. 603
Nashville, TN 37203
(615) 327–4521, (800) 344–4202
FAX: (615) 321–0731

American Leisure Network
(division of Morrie Trumble
& Assoc.)
1399 Fulton St., Ste. 403
New York, NY 10038
(212) 693–2633
FAX: (212) 571–1422

American Media
995 McMillan St.
Atlanta, GA 30318
(404) 873–3100

American Pie
P.O. Box 66455
Los Angeles, CA 90066
(213) 391–4088

American Radio Network
5287 W. Sunset Blvd.
Los Angeles, CA 90027
(213) 464–4580

American Radio Networks
423 New Karner Rd., Ste. 6
Albany, NY 12205
(518) 869–4386
FAX: (518) 869–8706

Anderson Media Services, Inc.
1465 Westwood Ave. SW
Atlanta, GA 30310
(404) 752–9353

The Answer
P.O. Box 4217
St. Louis, MO 63163
(314) 771–8271

AP Network News
AP Broadcast News Ctr. 6th Fl.
1825 K St. NW
Washington, DC 20006
(800) 821–4747

Stephen Arnold Music Production
2636 Walnut Hill, Ste. 100
Dallas, TX 75229
(214) 351–0291
FAX: (214) 352–8093

Toby Arnold & Associates
3234 Commander Dr.
Carrollton, TX 75006
(214) 661–8201, (800) 527–5335
FAX: (214) 250–6014

Association of Unity Churches
P.O. Box 610
Lee's Summit, MO 64063
(816) 524–7414
FAX: (816) 251–3561

Attic Witt
1520 First Ave., Ste. 2A
New York, NY 10021
(212) 535-5645

Audio Creations
801 Starmount Ave., NW
Roanoke, VA 24019
(703) 563-8100

Dale Baglo Broadcast, Inc.
825 Broughton St.
Victoria, BC
Canada, V8W 1E5
(604) 386-1131
FAX: (604) 386-5775

Bailey Broadcasting Service
3151 Cahuenga Blvd. W., Ste.
Los Angeles, CA 90068
(213) 969-0011
FAX: (213) 969-8474

Barrett Associates Inc.
3205 Production Ave.
Oceanside, CA 92054
(619) 433-5600
FAX: (619) 433-1590

Beethoven Satelite Network
c/o WFMT
303 E. Wacker Dr.
Chicago, IL 60601
(312) 565-5005
FAX: (312) 565-5169

Beige Cave Comedy Network
6404 Hollywood Blvd., #415
Hollywood, CA 90028
(213) 469-0157

Belly Laffs
1 Riverview Drive
North Providence, RI 02904

Frank Bennett Media Ventures
3131 Homestead Road, #17K
Santa Clara, LA 95051
(408) 247-0762

Best of the Oldies Radio Network
15651 Dickens St. #115
Encino, CA 91436
(818) 905-9388

Beyond Bourbon Jazz Productions
P.O. Box 169 MO
Milford, CT 06460
(203) 877-3690

BM Productions
P.O. Box 175
Northford, CT 06472
(203) 388-3548

Mike Boyd Funeral Planning Consultant
P.O. Box 100043
Ft. Lauderdale, FL 33310-0043
(305) 735-5851

Bonneville Broadcasting System
4080 Commercial Ave.
Northbrook, IL 60062
(800) 631-1600
FAX: (312) 291 0841

Bradbury Communications (BRADCOM)
Unit 103-333, 2210 E. Highland
San Bernardino, CA 92404
(714) 876-2911

Bradley Communications, Inc.
101 West Baltimore Ave.
Lansdowne, PA 19050
(215) 259-1070
FAX: (215) 284-3704

Brainstorm Productions, Inc.
3731 W. 165
Cleveland, OH 44111
(216) 371–3534

The Breeze
1069 10th Ave., SE
Minneapolis, MN 55414
(800) 367–2811, (612) 378–1254
FAX: (612) 378–2546

Dick Brescia Associates
17 Appletree Ln
Norwalk, CT 06850

Broadcast Programming, Inc.
2211 Fifth Ave.
Seattle, WA 98121
(206) 728–2741, (800) 426–9082
FAX: (206) 441–6582

The Broadcasting Connection
9 S.W. Monroe Parkway #1290
Lake Oswego, OR 97035
(503) 652–2030

Brown Bag Productions
4134 S. Eudora St.
Englewood, CO 80110
(303) 756–9949
FAX: (303) 759–8213

James Paul Brown Entertainment
6700 Centinela Ave., Ste. 100
Culver City, CA 90230
(800) 345–2354
FAX: (213) 398–7416

Bullet Productions
120 N. Victory, Ste. 102
Burbank, CA 91502
(818) 846–8200
FAX: (818) 846–9870

Business News Broadcasting
50 Milk Street, 15th fl.
Boston, MA 02109
(617) 482–5380

Business Radio Network
888 Garden of the Gods Road
Colorado Springs, CO 80907
(800) 873–3344
FAX: (719) 528–5170

The Bustany Biggs Company
517 Sinclair
Glendale, CA 91206
(818) 500–9246

Cable Car Productions
5054 Golden Drive
San Jose, CA 95129
(408) 255–0358

Cadena Radio Centro
60 E. 42nd St. Ste. 1431
New York, NY 10165
(212) 682–0330

Carney Productions
320 S. Arnaz Dr., Ste. 105
Los Angeles, CA 90048
(213) 278–8142

Cat Trax, Inc.
309 West End Lane
Knoxville, TN 37919
(615) 584–2877

CBN Radio Network
CBN Center
Virginia Beach, VA 23463
(800) 777–2346
FAX: (804) 424–7777

CBS Radio Networks
51 W. 52nd St.
New York, NY 10019
(212) 975–4227
FAX: (212) 975–3981

Chart Facts
117 W. Harrison Bldg., 6th Floor
Chicago, IL 60605
(800) 776–7770

The Cheat Sheet
P.O. Box 53023
Knoxville, TN 37950–3023
(615) 588–5444

Chicago Radio Syndicate, Inc.
1134 N. La Brea
Los Angeles, CA 90038
(800) 621–6949, (213) 462–4966

The Children's Health News Network
Children's Hospital National Medical Center
111 Michigan Avenue, N.W.
Washington, DC 20010
(202) 939–4500
FAX: (202) 939–4543

Christian Countdown America
P.O. Box 900
Wheaton, IL 60189
(312) 820–1369

Christian Countdown USA
CBN Radio Network
Virginia Beach, VA 23463
(804) 523–7108
FAX: (804) 523–7990

Christian Science Monitor Syndicate, Inc.
One Exeter Plaza
Boston, MA 02116
(617) 262–7770

Lita Cohen Radio Services
105 Forrest Avenue, Ste. 4
Narberth, PA 19072
(215) 668–0722
FAX: (215) 299–2150

Collins Broadcast Services
174 Kind Henry Court
Palatine, IL 60067
(312) 991–1522

Coltan Communications, Inc.
431 Post Rd. East, Ste. 727
Westport, CT 06880
(203) 817 0676

Comedy Warehouse/CW Media
P.O. Box 149
Hales Corners, WI 53130
(414) 529–5813
FAX: (414) 529–2746

Computer Sports World
1005 Elm St.
Boulder City, NV 89005
(800) 321–5562
FAX: (702) 294–1322

Concept Productions
1224 Coloma Way
Roseville, CA 95661
(916) 782–7754, (800) 348–4800
FAX: (916) 786–8304

Condor Communications
Box 45, Station Z
Toronto, ONT
M5N 2Z3 Canada
(416) 781–1047

Contemporary Comedy
5804 Twineing
P.O. Box 271043
Dallas, TX 75227
(214) 381–4779

Comtemporary Group
680 Craig Rd., Penthouse
St. Louis, MO 63141
(314) 567–9650
FAX: (314) 569–0760

Contemporary Radio Network
3301 Third Street
Moline, IL 61265
(309) 797–2510
FAX: (309) 797–2538

Continuum Broadcasting Network
345 W. 85th St., Ste. 46
New York, NY 10024
(212) 713-5165

Cooley-Strickland Management
P.O. Box 1727
Panama City, FL 32401
(904) 785-8844
FAX: (904) 785-7084

Copley Entertainment
30 Woods Grove
Westport, CT 06880
(203) 227-5400

Copley Radio Network
P.O. Box 190
San Diego, CA 92112
(619) 293-1818

Countdown USA
655 Redwood Highway, Ste. 285
Mill Valley, CA 94941
(415) 383-7302
FAX: (415) 383-7326

Country-Phonics
3805 H. Street
Eureka, CA 95501
(707) 443-9836

Covenant House
440 9th Ave., 10th Floor
New York, NY 10001-1607
(212) 330-0403
FAX: (212) 967-2187

Creative Radio Network
30961 W. Agoura Rd., Ste. 215
Westlake, CA 91361
(800) 392-9999, (818) 707-9011

Credit Union National Association
P.O. Box 431
Madison, WI 53701
(608) 231-4000
FAX: (608) 231-1869

Creeyadio
(Publishers of 'One To One')
P.O. Box 9787
Fresno, CA 93794
(209) 226-0558

CRN International
1125 Dixwell Ave.
Hamden, CT 06514
(203) 562-9400
FAX: (203) 773-1114

Ron Cutler Productions
1639 Westwood Blvd.
Los Angeles, CA 90024
(213) 478-2166
FAX: (213) 444-9311

Daily Briefs
P.O. Box 1016
Santa Monica, CA 90406
(213) 395-2736

The Daily Feed
1012 14th St. NW, 2nd Fl.
Washington, DC 20005
(202) 638-4222

D.B. Productions, Inc.
8 Greenlea Lane
Weston, CT 06883
(203) 227-5299
FAX: (203) 227-1325

DeWolfe Music Library
25 W. 45th St.
New York, NY 10036
(212) 382-0220
FAX: (212) 382-0278

Diamond Communications
2835 Smith Ave., #205
Baltimore, MD 21209
(301) 486-4624

Digital Programming, Inc.
P.O. Box 8006
Van Nuys, CA 91409
(818) 780-9780

Digital Radio Network
43 Broadway
Brooklyn, NY 11211
(718) 486-8788
FAX: (718) 486-5092

DIR Broadcasting Corp.
32 E. 57th St., 6th Fl.
New York, NY 10022
(212) 371-6850
FAX: (212) 888-8650

DMR Broadcast Consultants
P.O. Box 15039, Center City Plaza
Portland, ME 04101
(207) 878-3421
FAX: (207) 878-3514

Dow Jones Radio Network
200 Liberty St.
New York, NY 10281
(212) 416-2381
FAX: (212) 416-2232

Drake Chenault Enterprises, Inc.
2000 Randolph Rd. SE
Albuquerque, NM 87106
(505) 247-3303
FAX: (505) 247-9964

Eagle Media Productions, Ltd.
P.O. Box 430
North Salem, NY 10560
(914) 669-5277

Electric Weenie
Joke Service
P.O. Box 2715
Quincy, MA 02269
(617) 749-6900, (800) 225-5061
FAX: (617) 749-3691

Entertainment Radio Inc.
11684 Ventura Blvd., Ste. 589
Studio City, CA 91604
(818) 985-4807
FAX: (818) 763-3977

Everett Enterprises
P.O. Box 1327
Beverly Hills, CA 90213
(213) 285-8232

Excel Communications/Powerpipes
8960 Springbrook Dr. #220
Minneapolis, MN 55433-5852
(612) 784-3989

Far West Communications, Inc.
120 N. Victory Blvd., #106
Burbank, CA 91502
(818) 566-7003

Financial Broadcasting Network
2049 Century Park East, Suite 790
Los Angeles, CA 90067
(213) 556-4100
FAX: (213) 556-4175

John Mack Flanagen Broadcast Services
720 Thronhill
Colma, CA 94015

Focus on Youth, Inc.
P.O. Box 3035
Princeton, NJ 08543
(609) 452-1150
FAX: (609) 683-9091

For The People Foundation, Inc.
P.O. Box 101
Cedar Key, FL 32625
(904) 543-5648
FAX: (904) 543-5833

Gags R'Us
350 S. Figueroa
Ste. 117-740
Los Angeles, CA 90071

Galaxy-L.A. Air Force
Current Artist & Record Information
1097 D-Bar-K Drive
Durango, CO 81301
(303) 247–5082

Garlin Sound Enterprises
7021 Hatillo Ave.
Canoga Park, CA 91306
(818) 347–3902

Anita Garner
12050 Valleyheart Drive, #101
Studio City, CA 91604
(818) 506–7546

Gaylord Radio Services
2644 McGavock Pike
Nashville, TN 37214
(800) 637–1718

Ghostwriters Comedy Service
2301 Unity Ave. N.
Minneapolis, MN 55422
(612) 522–6256

Givens Radio Network
921 Douglas Avenue
Altamonte Springs, FL 32714
(407) 862–4101

Global Satellite Network
15477 Ventura Blvd., Ste. 300
Sherman Oaks, CA 91403
(818) 906–1888
FAX: (818) 906–9736

Gold Mine
Box 25989
Honolulu, HI 96825
(808) 395–7500, (808) 395–7501

Art Good's Jazz Trax
701 Kettner, Ste. 204
San Diego, CA 92101
(619) 233–9228
FAX: (619) 233–7950

Groma Corporation/Funny Fillers
565 Pearl St. Ste. 200
La Jolla, CA 92037
(619) 454–6626

D. Guardino
P.O. Box 880
Lenoir City, TN 37771
(615) 558–6201

Gull Publishing
P.O. Box 10926
Baltimore, MD 21234
(301) 444–5703

Gwenn's Kitchen Talk
3549 Laurashawn Lane
Escondido, CA 92026
(619) 741–8572

Happy Hare Radio Theatre
3344 Tennyson St.
San Diego, CA 92106
(619) 224–6229

Harry Turner's Originals, Inc.
P.O. Box 4
Spartanburg, SC 29304

Heavens Above
Box 885
Willoughby, OH 44094
(216) 951–0030

Hell Enterprises
P.O. Box 1372
Lancaster, PA 17603
(717) 299–5899

Hollywood Hotline
P.O. Box 2510
Sparks, NV 89432
(702) 331–0991

The Home Shopping Network
1587 U.S. Highway 19 South
Clearwater, FL 34625
(813) 572–8585

The Hook Factory
11939 NE Halsey
Portland, OR 97220
(503) 252-0315
FAX: (503) 253-4175

Hot Mix Radio Network
1920 E. 3rd St., Ste. 11
Tempe, AZ 85281
(602) 966-9900
FAX: (602) 921-7199

House of Music
5749 Creekside, #18
Orange, CA 92669
(714) 997-5309

Hype Ink
7805 Sunset Blvd., Ste. 206
Los Angeles, CA 90046
(213) 850-5755

In-Fisherman Communications Network
651 Edgewood Drive
Brawerd, MN 56401
(218) 829-8909

Info Bits
Box 112576
San Diego, CA 92111
(619) 279-3119

Innerview, Inc.
8913 W. Olympic Blvd., Ste. 201
Beverly Hills, CA 90211
(213) 652-8710

Inside Tract Productions
1128 Western, Ste. 1
Fairfield, CA 94533
(707) 425-1493

The International Lutheran Laymen's League
2185 Hampton Ave.
St. Louis, MO 63139
(314) 647-4900
FAX: (314) 647-6923

Interstate Satellite Network
1748 W. Katella
Orange, CA 92667
(714) 633-2020
FAX: (714) 997-0182

The Interview Factory
P.O. Box 615
Van Nuys, CA 91408
(818) 988-2045

JAM Creative Productions, Inc.
5454 Parkdale Dr.
Dallas, TX 75227
(214) 388-5454
FAX: (214) 381-4647

Jameson Broadcasting
1700 Connecticut Ave. NW, Ste. 402
Washington, DC 20009
(202) 328-3283
FAX: (202) 332-6810

The Jazz Life
705 Jerilyn Dr.
Charlotte, NC 28212
(704) 567-9782

Susan B. Anthony Jones
2408 Bainbridge St.
Richmond, VA 23225
(804) 231-9861

JoxFax
Box 2092
Adelaide 5001
Australia,

Matt Judge Comedy Service
3836 Front Sr., #101
San Diego, CA 93103
(619) 692–0896

Julio Productions
P.O. Box 70866
Las Vegas, NV 89109
(702) 361–2946

Just for Laughs Creative Services
P.O. Box 2333
Denton, TX 76202
(817) 382–2275

Kalamusic
4200 W. Main St.
Kalamazoo, MI 49007
(616) 385–5110, (800) 289-KALA
FAX: (616) 345–1436

Kaleidophonic Jazz
3805 H St.
Eureka, CA 95501
(707) 443–9836

Kaleidophonics
New Age Format Service
3805 H Street
Eureka, CA 95501
(707) 443–9836

Kamikazee Airways
3830 Central Ave., Ste. 211
Ft. Myers, FL 33901
(813) 275–8530

John Kane, English Psychic
181 N. Mill St., Ste. 9B
Lexington, KY 40507
(606) 259–1933

Kenetics Radio Entertainment
1122 Ocean Ave.
Brooklyn, NY 11230
(718) 859–6123

Kidsounds, Inc.
7515 Greenville, Ste. 405
Dallas, TX 75231

Knockers*!
P.O. Box 153
La Grange, IL 60525
(312) 579–9578

L.A.F. Productions
P.O. Box 10263
Burbank, CA 91510
(818) 848–1497

Laffline
117 W. Harrison Bldg., Ste. 640
Chicago, IL 60605

Mark Larson Programming & Production
P.O. Box 2424
El Cajon, CA 92021
(619) 579–0967
FAX: (619) 279–7676

LaughLine
717 4th St., Ste. A
Des Moines, IA 50309

Andy Lea's Reel Thing
1003 Stanyan Street
San Francisco, CA 94117
(415) 563–5573

Little Ricky Rocko Productions
4949 S.W. Macadam
Portland, OR 97201
(503) 226–0100

Low Noise Productions
10 Ferndale
Fenton, MO 63026
(314) 343–9251

Maccabees/Whorf Productions
239 Pilgrim
Birmingham, MI 48009
(313) 433–3742

Marleigh Radio Syndicators
505 Fifth Ave., Ste. 1602
New York, NY 10017
(212) 370 0110

Marshall Arts
8847 Cleary Blvd.
Plantation, FL 33324
(305) 370–0529

Martin Communications
P.O. Box 32681
Baltimore, MD 21209
(301) 764–8550

McGhan Radio Productions
7441 Palo Vista Dr.
Los Angeles, CA 90046
(213) 850–7417
FAX: (213) 876–5477

Media America
11 West 42nd Street, 27th Fl.
New York, NY 10036
(212) 302–1100
FAX: (212) 302–6024

Media General Broadcast Services, Inc.
2714 Union Extended
Memphis, TN 38112
(901) 320–4340
FAX: (901) 320–4229

MegaloMedia Productions
1959 Grace Avenue, Ste. 206
Hollywood, CA 90068
(213) 874–2863

Melcor Broadcasting Company
380 Lexington Avenue
New York, NY 10168
(212) 972–1030

Metro Network, Inc.
2300 M. St. N.W., #800
Washington, DC 20037
(202) 331–7307

Metro Traffic Control
2700 Post Oak Blvd., Ste. 1400
Houston, TX 77056
(713) 621–2800
FAX: (713) 622–9071

Charles Michelson & Sons
9350 Wilshire Blvd.
Beverly Hills, CA 90212
(213) 278–4546, (800) 648–4546
FAX: (213) 271–3040

Robert Michelson Inc.
127 W. 26th St.
New York, NY 10001
(212) 243–2702
FAX: (212) 691–5531

MJI Broadcasting Inc.
666 Fifth Ave., 34th Floor
New York, NY 10103
(212) 245–5010
FAX: (212) 586–1090

MNN Radio Networks, Inc.
45 East Seventh St.
St. Paul, MN 55101
(612) 290–1234
FAX: (612) 290–1260

Moss Broadcasting Comm.
575 Main St., Ste. 512
New York, NY 10044
(212) 644–2530
FAX: (212) 319–4182

Motorcycle Touring Live
1081 N. Elmwood Drive
Aurora, IL 60506

Mr. Hollywood
2007 Vail, Ste. 3
Rendondo Beach, CA 90278
(213) 542–9186

**M.R.N. Radio
(Motor Racing Network)**
P.O. Drawer S
Daytona Beach, FL 32015
(904) 254-6760

Muddy Mitch Productions
4315 Azalea, Ste. 220
Lisle, IL 60532
(312) 971-3890

Music Director Programming Svc.
P.O. Box 51978
Indian Orchard, MA 01151
(413) 783-4626

Music Media International
Zaartweg 129
Hilversum 12175N
Holland,
011-31-3547057

Music Of Your Life/Fairwest
6020 Cornerstone Ct., Ste. 100
San Diego, CA 92121
(619) 552-0777

**Music Unlimited
Productions/Consultation**
763 Taft Dr., Ste. G
Arlington, TX 76011
(817) 261-3520

Musica En Flor
Calle E F-14, Villanova
Rio Piedras, PR 00926
(809) 720-1545

Musical Starstreams
P.O. Box 44
Mill Valley, CA 94942
(415) 383-7827

Musicworks, Inc.
P.O. Box 111390
Nashville, TN 37211
(615) 790-1200, (800) 251-9000

Mutual Broadcasting System
1755 S. Jefferson Davis Hwy.
Arlington, VA 22202
(703) 685-2000
FAX: (703) 685-2145

Narwood Productions Inc.
40 E. 49th St.
New York, NY 10017
(212) 755-3320

National Black Network
10 Columbus Circle
New York, NY 10019
(212) 586-0610, (212) 307-0635

National Wildlife Federation
1400 16th St. NW
Washington, DC 20036
(202) 797-6850
FAX: (202) 797-6646

NBC Radio Network
1700 Broadway
New York, NY 10019
(212) 237-2500
FAX: (212) 245-6219

New Century Broadcasting
444 Gulf of Mexico Dr.
Longboat Key, FL 33548
(813) 383-8881

Newsletter Services
1545 New York Ave. NE
Washington, DC 20002
(202) 529-5700

Newsmaker Interviews
8217 Beverly Blvd.
Los Angeles, CA 90048
(213) 655-2793

Non-Stop Productions
915 West 100 South
Salt Lake City, UT 84104
(801) 531-0060

North America One
P.O. Box 642
Richland Center, WI 53581
(608) 647-6387
FAX: (608) 647-3065

North American Network
2316 18th Street NW
Washington, DC 20009
(202) 265-3689
FAX: (202) 265-2294

Nostalgia Notes
P.O. Box 414
Hingham, MA 02043
(617) 749-9189

NUAUD Corp.
183-11 Hillside Ave., Ste. 8-L
Jamaica, NY 11432
(718) 657-7657

O'Connor Creative Services
P.O. Box 5432
Playa del Rey, CA 90296
(213) 827-2527
FAX: (213) 301-3363

O'Liners
11060 Cashmere St.
Los Angeles, CA 90049
(213) 479-1767

An Ocean of Comedy
P.O. Box 10523
Zephyr Cove, NV 89448
(916) 542-1185

Olympia Broadcasting Networks
22 North Euclid
St. Louis, MO 63108
(314) 361-2000
FAX: (314) 361-2393

On The Radio Broadcasting
400 Sunridge St.
Playa del Rey, CA 90293
(213) 306-8009
FAX: (213) 305-1467

Pacific Audio Makers
1999 Temple, Unit B
P.O. Box 4087
Long Beach, CA 90802
(213) 597-8344

Parkway/Muse, Inc.
1090 Taft St.
Rockville, MD 20850
(301) 294-0790, (800) 247-6040

Byron Paul Voices
P.O. Box 1016
Santa Monica, CA 90406
(213) 395-2736

PD Newsletter
1400 Washington Memorial Dr., Ste. 205
St. Cloud, MN 56301

Pennsylvania Network
260 South Broad Street, Ste. 200
Philadelphia, PA 19102
(215) 732-7100, (800) 222-2191

Phantastic Phunnies
Topical Comedy One-Liners
1343 Strafford Dr.
Kent, OH 44240
(216) 673-5095

PIA
680 N. Lakeshore Dr., Ste. 800
Chicago IL 60611
(312) 943-8888
FAX: (312) 943-5464

Planet Productions
P.O. Box 3889
Austin, TX 78764
(512) 482-8552

Premiere Radio Networks
6255 Sunset Blvd., Penthouse
Hollywood, CA 90028
(213) 467–2346
FAX: (213) 467–9540

Pro Audio Makers
1999 Temple, Unit B
P.O. Box 4087
Long Beach, CA 90802
(213) 597–8344

Professional Radio Networks
197 W. 12th Ave
Eugene, OR 97401
(503) 687–2068, (800) 882–3883
FAX: (503) 686–0248

Program Distributors
P.O. Drawer 1737
Jonesboro, AR 72403
(501) 972–5884

ProMedia
170 Ludlow Ave
Northvale, NJ 07647
(201) 768–7900, (800) 782–0700
FAX: (201) 784–0077

PUNCHLINERS
2714 Stateview Dr.
Toledo, OH 43609
(419) 382–7572

Pure Rock Network
6577 E. Camino Vista #4
Anaheim, CA 92807
(714) 974–6841

Quantum Concepts Unlimited
12262 Hythe Street
Moreno Valley, CA 92387
(714) 683–2161

Radio & Television Commission
6350 W. Freeway
Ft. Worth, TX 76150
(817) 737–4011, (800) 433–5757

The Radio Almanac
107 Jensen Circle
W. Springfield, MA 01089
(413) 737–7600

Radio AMEX/AMEX Business Talk
86 Trinity Place
New York, NY 10006
(212) 306–1637
FAX: (212) 306–1488

Radio Cinema
11300 4th St. North, Ste. 140
St. Petersburg, FL 33716
(813) 576–4594
FAX: (813) 578–1348

The Radio Comedy Company
Baker Sound Studios
1821 Ranstead St.
Philadelphia, PA 19103
(215) 567–0430

Radio Express
3575 Cahuenga Blvd. W., Ste. 390
Los Angeles, CA 90068
(213) 850–1003
FAX: (213) 874–7753

Radio Links
7038 Grasswood Ave.
Malibu, CA 90265
(213) 457–5358
FAX: (213) 457–5358

Radio Networks, Inc.
P.O. Box 738
Syracuse, NY 13214
(800) 553–5688

The Radio Newsreel
3421 M Street NW, Ste. 321
Washington, DC 20007
(703) 534–4665

Radio Program Services/Barrett Associates
3205 Productions Avenue
Oceanside, CA 92054
(619) 433–5600
FAX: (619) 433–1590

Radio Programming & Management, Inc.
4198 Orchard Lake Rd.
Orchard Lake, MI 48033
(313) 681–2660, (800) 521–2537
FAX: (313) 681–3936

Radio Today Entertainment
211 W. 56th St., Ste. 3A
New York, NY 10019
(212) 581–3962
FAX: (212) 459–9343

Radio Ventures
7 E. Cherry St.
Floral Park, NY 11001
(516) 358–2250

radioWAVE
1040 Greenwich St.
San Francisco, CA 94133
(415) 771–5886

Radio Weather Network
8312 Florida Street
Ste. 207
Baton Rouge, LA 70806

Radiocraft, Inc.
P.O. Box U
Southborough, MA 01745
(508) 485–3500
FAX: (508) 480–8310

Radioworks
5900 Wilshire, Ste. 1400
Los Angeles, CA 90036
(213) 938–4700

REMN Communications Corp.
2 W. 45th St.
New York, NY 10036
(212) 302–9120

Renaissance Radio Theater
4902 Firwood Dr.
Ft. Wayne, IN 46835
(219) 426–4401

Rex
285 Riverside Avenue, Ste. 300
Westport, CT 06880
(203) 222–5858
FAX: (203) 222–5864

Roberts & Bie
6255 Sunset Blvd., Ste. 110
Los Angeles, CA 90028
(818) 760–4313

Rock Air Productions
12021 Wilshire Blvd., Ste. 535
Los Angeles, CA 90025
(213) 471–0938

RPMC, Inc.
17514 Ventura Blvd., Ste. 202
Encino, CA 91316
(818) 501–7762
FAX: (818) 501–8848

Carol Rushman & Company
6290 N. Port Washington Rd.
Glendale, WI 53217
(141) 962–5228

Sacred Heart Program, Inc.
3900 Westminster Pl.
St. Louis, MO 63108
(314) 533–0320

Salsbury/Ziglar Marketing Associates
81 Church Street
Lenox, MA 01240
(413) 637–2631

Satellite Music Network
12655 N. Central Expressway, Ste. 600
Dallas, TX 75243
(800) 527-4892, (214) 991-9200
FAX: (214) 991-1071

The Senate Today Newsfeed
405 Hart Senate Office Bldg.
Washington, DC 20510
(800) 736-1001, (800) 736-2255

Shade Communications
530 Ellsworth Avenue
New York, NY
(212) 792-7576

Shaw-Spelling Associates
520 Broadway, 4th Fl.
Santa Monia, CA 90401
(213) 458-2011
FAX: (213) 394-8852

Sheridan Broadcasting Network
1 Times Square Plaza, 18th Fl.
New York, NY 10036
(212) 575-0099

Sheridan Broadcasting Networks
411 7th Ave.
PIttsburgh, PA 15219
(412) 281-6751
FAX: (412) 391-3559

Sixty-Second Preview
285 Riverside Avenue, Ste. 300
Westport, CT 06880
(203) 222-5859
FAX: (203) 222-5864

SJP Enterprises
P.O. Box 491097
Los Angeles, CA 90049
(213) 471-0609
FAX: (213) 471-0877

SJS Entertainment
800 Second Ave., 13th Fl.
New York, NY 10017
(800) 548-4757
FAX: (212) 867-6113

Denny Somach Productions
812 W. Darby Rd.
Havertown, PA 19083
(215) 446-7100
FAX: (215) 446-7721

Soundscapes
1187 Coast Village Rd., Ste. 1-117
Santa Barbara, CA 93108
(805) 965-3581
FAX: (805) 969-1725

The Source
1700 Broadway
New York, NY 10019
(212) 237-2500
FAX: (212) 245-6219

Sportcom Associates
Motor Sports Radio
1285 Zevan Road
Johnson City, NY 13790-9715
(607) 770-9165
FAX: (607) 722-8093

Sports Ticker
Harborside Financial Center
600 Plaza 2
Jersey City, NJ 07311
(201) 309-1260
FAX: (201) 860-9742

Sportsline USA
300 Broadway, Ste. 8
San Francisco, CA 94133
(415) 434-8300
FAX: (415) 391-2569

Star Communications
P.O. Box 644
Boston, MA 02128
(617) 569-7467
FAX: (617) 561-1379

StarDate
University of Texas
McDonald Observatory
Austin, TX 78712
(512) 471-5285

Starmagic Radio
755 River Road
Teaneck, NJ 07666
(201) 836-5999
FAX: (201) 837-8979

Starstream Communications
9800 Richmond, Ste. 300
Houston, TX 77042
(713) 781-0781
FAX: (713) 781-4721

Stateman Broadcasting Network
8121 Georgia Ave., Ste., 701
Silver Spring, MD 20910
(301) 587-6800

Kris Stevens Enterprises
14241 Ventura Blvd., Ste. 204
Sherman Oaks, CA 91423
(818) 981-8255
FAX: (818) 990-4350

Sun Networks, Inc.
1201 W. Hillsborough Ave.
Tampa, FL 33603
(813) 238-3145
FAX: (813) 237-2238

SuperRadio Network
World Trade Center, Ste. 400
Boston, MA 02110
(617) 266-2900
FX: (617) 439-5305

Supertrax Production Services
7827 Farrell
Amarillo, TX 79121
(806) 352 7503

Syndicom
P.O. Box 12837
San Luis Obispo, CA 93406
(805) 543-9214
FAX: (805) 543-9243

Talknet
1700 Broadway
New York, NY 10019
(212) 237-2500
FAX: (212) 245-2250

TD Productions
28788 Piedmont Dr.
Farmington Hills, MI 48331
(313) 344-0263

Techsonics on CD
709 Shadowfield Ct.
Chesapeake, VA 23320
(804) 547-4000

Tele-Joke
4555 N. Pershing Avenue, Ste. 33-376
Stockton, CA 95207
(209) 476-1511

TelePrograms, Inc.
8500 Melrose, Ste. 213
Los Angeles, CA 90069
(213) 854-4475
FAX: (213) 854-5979

Tony Rizzini
RR#1, Saw Mill Rd.
Chepachet, RI 02814
(401) 949-4142

Tony Weasel Report from Hollywood
Warner Hollywood Studios
1041 N. Formosa, #108-B
Hollywood, CA 90046
(213) 850-2505

Ric Tower's Hot Sheets
One Life Comedy Service
P.O. Box 4858
St. Louis, MO 63108
(314) 225–7110

Transmedia
350 Pacific
San Francisco, CA 94111
(415) 956–3118

Transorbital Productions, Ltd.
557 Street Lane
Leeds W. Yorkshire, L517 6JA
England 011–44532–87886

Transtar Radio Network
660 Southpointe Ct., Ste. 200
Colorado Springs, CO 80906
(719) 576–2620
FAX: (719) 576–3438

Transtar Special Programming
6430 Sunset Blvd., Ste. 401
Los Angeles, CA 90028
(213) 460–6383
FAX: (213) 460–6341

Tribune Radio Network
435 North Michigan Ave.
Chicago, IL 60611
(312) 222–5152

Trivia Werks
497 Walmar Dr.
Bay Village, OH 44140
(216) 892–8509
FAX: (216) 892 8503

Morrie Trumble & Associates, Inc.
139 Fulton St., Ste. 403
New York, NY 10038
(212) 693–2633
FAX: (212) 571–1422

Unidyne Communications
2250 Columbia St., Ste. 100
San Diego, CA 92101
(619) 239–8911
FAX: (619) 239–4714

U.P.I. Radio Network
United Press International
1400 Eye St. NW
Washington, DC 20005
(202) 898–8200
FAX: (202) 842–3625

United Stations Programming
2000 15th St. N., Ste. 200
Arlington, VA 22201
(703) 276–2900
FAX: (703) 276–2919

United Stations Radio Networks
1440 Broadway
New York, NY 10018
(212) 575–6100

USA Radio Network
2290 Springlake, Ste. 107
Dallas, TX 75234
(214) 484–3900
FAX: (214) 243–3489

USA TODAY Decisionline
& Lifestyle Reports
P.O. Box 450
Washington, DC 20044
(800) 222–0990
FAX: (202) 243–0150

Vanda Productions
302 E. Chestnut St.
Hartselle, AL 35640
(205) 773–5201

Van Winkel Syndication
P.O. Box 427
Portland, OR 97207
(503) 591–1482

The Very Best Videos
285 Riverside Avenue, Ste. 300
Westport, CT 06880
(203) 222-5860
FAX: (203) 222-5864

Veterans Radio Network, Inc.
P.O. Box 658
Moline, IL 61265
(309) 797-2510

Don Vogel
115 Roslyn Dr.
Concord, CA 94518
(415) 827-2382

Wall Street Journal Radio Network
200 Liberty St.
New York, NY 10281
(212) 416-2381
FAX: (212) 416-2232

Jim Warren Entertainment
7080 Hollywood Blvd., Ste. 1002
Hollywood, CA 90028
(213) 465-5111

WB Enterprises
Box 385
Lamar, CO 81052

Weather Scan
P.O. Box 164
Orleand, PA 19075
(215) 887-3321

Ken Webb Enterprises, Inc.
P.O. Box 548
Wheatley Heights, NY 11798
(516) 491-5368, (212) 681-8840
FAX: (516) 491-1354

Weedeck Radio Network
1516 Crossroads of the World
Hollywood, CA 90028
(800) 548-7474, (213) 462-5922

Weemaway Amusement Co.
5981 S. Tabor St.
Littleton, CO 80127

Western Front Broadcasting
115 N. Vine Street
Anaheim, CA 92805
(714) 772-5729

Westwood One Radio Networks
9540 Washington Blvd.
Culver City, CA 90232
(213) 840-4000
FAX: (213) 204-4375

WFMT Fine Arts Network
303 E. Wacker Dr.
Chicago, IL 60601
(312) 565-5005
FAX: (312) 565-5169

Wheeler-Lewis Productions
2899 Agoura Rd., Ste. 390
Westlake Village, CA 92361
(805) 492-0546

Gary Whiteaker Corp.
P.O. Box 307
Belleville, IL 62222
(618) 476-7771

Willy's Comedy Shack & Burger Emporium
11A Galley Ave
Toronto, Ontario, CN M6R 1G9
(416) 363-0997
FAX: (416) 363-9090

Winton Communications, Inc.
4102 W. Linebaugh Ave., Ste. 210
Tampa, FL 33624
(813) 962-2336
FAX: (813) 960-1393

Bob Wood Organization
4778 Renovo Way
San Diego, CA 92124
(619) 565-2006

World Beat
1463 Sacramento St., Ste. 1A
San Francisco, CA 94109
(415) 474–7773

World Space Report
P.O. Box 3803
Stamford, CT 06905
(203) 329–1992, (800) 622–1992

Wright Radio Services
The Wright Stuff-Joke Service
P.O. Box 582
Felton, DE 19943
(302) 284–4400

Rob Young
842 Sunset Blvd., #14
Kenner, LA 70065
(504) 468–1421

Chapter 9

Conclusion

The music industry has never been bigger. According to the RIAA, one of the industry's major associations, It is currently an industry which generates over $4 billion dollars annually. With the advent of the new technologies—compact digital discs, digital audio tape recorders and further integration of the computer as a vital part in the making and playing of music—this growth will certainly continue.

Records are now easier to produce in the studio thanks to this technology. It is now possible for a single musician to play all parts in a composition using digital sampling instruments and multi-track recorders. This same musician can also record the various tracks of a composition using digital tape recorders to produce a technically superior product for resale. The future of this industry appears to be bright as many of these devices are now within the budget of a great many consumers. As history has always demonstrated, as a technology evolves, the price of the existing technology becomes lower thus, more affordable. This trend could possibly mean that in the near future all consumers of music will have the ability to become a record production company with full production capability only having to concern themselves with the problems of distribution and mass manufacturing. As the current personal computer music software programs continue to evolve from their present state of giving consumers, with little or no musical training, the ability to compose and write music, the industry may begin to see every consumer as a potential music publisher, every customer as a competitor. As Digital Audio Recorders become even more of a reality and more affordable then even the duplication process of this consumer/produced music will cease to be a problem. Since every copy of a digitally recorded production transferred to a digital cassette is, in every respect, a perfect copy, the process of high quality tape duplication may soon be as easy as turning on a television set. The next cottage industry may well be neighborhood, city, or regional record companies operated by consumers from their basements, dens, bedrooms or wherever the equipment will fit.

The music industry has certainly come a long way—from Edison's first analog recording of 'Mary had a little lamb' to digital technology . . . from "Your Hit Parade" on network radio to MTV and VH-1 . . . from format radio to format television. Add the technology of Low Power Television, and we may eventually see these neighborhood record companies also become the neighborhood music channel as well. Low Power Television with its limited coverage may well have the same meaning to the new music entrepreneur as Top 40 radio had for the old ones. Eventually we will see another new technology unfold—D.B.S.—Direct Broadcast Satellite. This technology giving the user of this system the unique ability to reach a very highly defined geographical area thus a discrete target audience via satellite with the only equipment required by the consumer being a very small receiving dish within the home, could mean that the new music entrepreneur will now have the ability to make the music, broadcast the music directly to the new consumers via DBS and thus become a 'basement' radio station with unlimited reach.

All of this may sound futuristic but the technology to make it all possible is here. With all of the mechanical pieces in place all that will be needed are consumers informed and educated about the workings of this industry, which gets us to the point of this book.

In order to be able to appreciate and improve upon the existing ways of the industry one must first have a working knowledge of it. By understanding how the music industry evolved to its present state and by understanding how the industry components mesh to form this machine of commerce perhaps the student will find a place where his/her skills will fit. Historically, the inner workings of the industry have been acquired from those within the industry and given to those few persons exposed to those within. Many of the latest writings now are addressing this sharing, or lack of sharing, of knowledge with the general public. The music industry is not mystical and, in many instances, has not been practical but the industry survives. Music is a vital part of the American lifestyle as evidenced by the fact that the United States is the world's largest music consumer. The Music Industry will continue to grow as all statistical indicators point to the fact that the makeup of the record buying public is changing . . . as the country grows older, as the 'baby boomers' become middle-aged, they continue to listen to and buy music. Even the children of the boomers—the boomlets—will have tremendous buying power well into the next century. This means that the marketplace is healthy and, from all indications, will stay that way. The recent example of this market vitality was seen in Michael Jackson's *Thriller* album. The phenomenal sales of this record—over 40 million units to date—indicate that as the years go on, a hit record still has the ability to appeal to a broad spectrum audience.

As the music industry continues to evolve, the consumer will do the same. At this writing, the major record companies have made decisions that truly are indicative of the future. Companies have decided, among other things, that it is now no longer in their best interest to service radio stations with vinyl 45 singles as promotion items as most play now occurs from compact disk albums and singles; digital audio tape for the consumer will happen with a compromise made between the manufacturers of the machines and the record companies wherein these machines will, indeed, have the ability to record and make copies of compact discs but will come equipped with a device to prevent the duplication of digital tapes. Jukeboxes are begining to phase out vinyl records in favor of digital discs.

MTV, music televison is struggling for a larger share of the audience as other broadcast outlets are now using the same formula in reaching a core target audience of video music consumers. VH-1—sister channel to MTV—originally intended to reach an older demographic with music is considering accomplishing this without the services of 'video d.j.'s' as they are now seen as probable tune out factors in the channel's quest for viewers. Television is beginning to sound like format radio which again bears out the reality of the industry's proclivity to change . . . but not really.

Format radio is seeking more personality as the 'ultimate' solution to finding and keeping new listeners . . . personality radio is seeking more structure in order to prevent the personalities from causing the audience to be driven away.

However, the question persists: can the industry, under careful historical examination, offer any degree of predictability. The answer usually is both yes and no. This industry, like every other, has good and bad periods. Can history be examined to predict hits? If the answer was yes every music historian would be worth his weight in gold—and platinum!! Should the industry be investigated? Most certainly but at the end of the day the only definite prediction will be that the more things change . . . the more they stay the same.

Appendix A

Bibliography

Alten, Stanley R. *Audio in Media 2nd Ed.* Wadsworth Publishing Co. Belmont, Ca.

Atwan, Robert Orton, Barry, Vesterman, Wm. *American Mass Media* 3rd ed. 1986 Randon House. N.Y.

Baskerville, David. *Music Business Handbook and Career Guide.* 1985. The Sherwood Company. Denver, Co.

Blume, Daniel. *Making It in Radio.* 1983. Continental Media. Hartford, Conn.

Chapple, Steve and Garofolo, Reebee. *Rock and Roll is Here to Pay* Nelson-Hall Publications, Chicago, Ill.

Denisoff, R. Serge. *Inside MTV.* 1988. Transaction Press, New Brunswick, New Jersey

Denisoff, R. Serge. *Solid Gold.* 1975 Transaction Press, New Brunswick, New Jersey

Denisoff, R. Serge. *Tarnished Gold.* 1986. Transaction Press, New Brunswick, New Jersey

Gillete, Charlie. *The Sound of the City.* 1972. Dell Books. New York, N.Y.

Hall, Claude. *This Business of Radio Programming* 1975. Billboard Publications

Hurst, Walter E. *The Record Industry Book.* Arts Press Entertainment Industry Series

Oakley, Giles. *The Devil's Music: A History of the Blues.* 1976. H.B.J. New York, N.Y.

Pember, Donald. *Mass Media and Society*

Rachlin, Harvey. *The Encyclopedia of the Popular Music Business.* 1981. Harper and Row, New York

Shemel, Sidney and Krasilovosky, William M. 1985. Billboard Publications, New York, N.Y.

Shemel, Sidney and Krasilovosky, William M. *This Business of Music* 1985. Billboard Publications, New York, N.Y.

Southern, Eileen. *The Music of Black Americans.* 1971. W.W. Norton Co. New York, N.Y.

Fornatale, Peter and Mills Joshua. *Radio in the Television Age* Overlook Press Woodstock, N.Y.

Appendix B

Glossary

A

Advance—A fee paid to an artist as part of the royalty compensation package.

A. and R. Artists and Repertoire—Department of record company responsible for talent acquisition.

AFM. American Federation of Musicians—Trade union for television, radio and record performers.

AFTRA.—American Federation of Television and Radio Artists.

AGMA.—American Guild of Musical Artists.

AGVA.—American Guild of Variety Artists.

AM.—In electronic communications, a type of radio station whose signal is encoded by its carrier wave being *A*mplitude *M*odulated.

ANALOG—the electronic representation of a sound wave as a physical copy.

AOR.—Album Oriented Rock—a radio format usually consisting of various selections from rock albums.

ARB—Arbitron. Formerly the American Research Bureau. A television ratings company.

A.S.C.A.P. American Society of Composers, Authors and Publishers—America's oldest performing rights organization.

B

Birch Report—A radio ratings service.

Billboard—A leading trade industry magazine whose charts are used extensively by industry professionals.

BMA. Black Music Association—Trade organization representing Black performers.

BMI Broadcast Music, Inc.—American performing rights society.

Bootlegging—The illegal practice of recording an artist without permission and then offering the recording for sale.

C

C.D. Compact Disc.—A format for recordings using electronic digital technology.

Chart—Trade newspaper listing of records according to their relative popularity. Charts are an important barometer of a record's success.

CHR Contemporary Hit Radio.—A radio programing scheme much like Top 40. (see top 40)

CMA. Country Music Association—Trade organization known best for its country music awards program.

Contractor—The person, required by union contracts, to hire performers. This person is paid double scale . . . twice the union agreed upon single session rate for performers.

Cooperative Advertising-coop—An advertising scheme wherein a record company will share advertising costs of a product with a retailer. This becomes shared advertising with mutual benefits.

Counterfeiting—The illegal practice and process of copying a record (tape, c.d.) and then offering the copies for sale as originals.

Creative Services—Department within a record company responsible for album covers, posters and other visual sales tools.

Cross-collateralization—A clause within recording contracts allowing the profits from each successful recording to be used to pay for the expenses of unsuccessful recordings under the same contractual arrangement.

Crossover—A record intended for a specialized audience but finds success with other such audiences.

Cut out—A record or tape that has reached the sales saturation in the marketplace. These items are them sold at tremendous discounts to dealers with the expectation that additional profit will be realized after the maximum of new record sales point.

D

D.A.T.—Digital Audio Tape—A high quality recording/playback technology which uses pulse-code modulation to encode information onto a tape.

DBS—Direct Broadcast Satellite.—A method of program distribution which uses a high power satellite to transmit a signal to a highly defined coverage area.

DeFacto Network—A broadcast scheme wherein independent broadcast stations, not affiliated with a dedicated network, provide access to program suppliers for limited times.

Demographic—A statistical representation of an audience segment.

Digital—In recording and playback the technology wherein the encoded/decoded information is represented as a binary code, series of ones and zeros.

Doubling—A recording technique which requires a musician or singer to perform the same art twice on a different recording track.

E

Electromagnetic recording—the process in which program material is magnetically encoded onto a medium usually magnetic tape.

F

FCC—Federal Communications Commission. Government agency responsible for licensing all radio, television, satellite, and telephone communications.

FTC—Federal Trade Commission.—Government agency responsible for regulation of interstate commerce.

F.M.—Frequency Modulation.—In radio communication a station whose carrier signal is changed by changes in source frequency.

Free Goods—Records supplied by manufacturers at no charge as an incentive for sales.

G

Grand Rights—a licence issued by a copyright holder through its performing rights organization for use of material in musical drama.

Grammy—Award given annually by NARAS

H

HFA—The Harry Fox Agency—organization owned and operated by the National Music Publishers Association. The HFA's primary function is the issue and overseeing of mechanical licenses.

House Producer—A producer who is usually an employee of a record company.

House Music—A style of mixing music wherein different artists and albums are combined to produce a continuous dance track.

I

IBEW—International Brotherhood of Electrical Workers—Trade union whose members include engineers and technicians.

Independent—Record company—A record company that does not provide full manufacturing and distribution services. See Majors.

Independent—Promotion Person—Free-lance professional used by companies to augment its own staff.

Independent—Producer—Free-lance creative production executive hired by companies on a project by project basis.

J

Jukebox—A coin operated electronic record player.

L

List price—The retail price of a product. (as compared to wholesale)

M

Master—The finished production reduced to a two track tape. Subsequent copies are made in several formats for resale.

Mechanical—a license given by a copyright owner authorizing the reproduction of records and tapes.

Mom and Pop—Very small retail outlets.

N

NAC—New Age—A radio format identified by an almost jazz-like presentation.

NAB—National Association of Broadcasters—Trade Association whose members include radio and television station owners and managers.

NABET—National Association of Broadcast Employees and Technicians—A trade union that represents, primarily, broadcast technicians.

NARAS. National Academy of Recording Arts and Sciences—Trade association for the music industry known best for its presentation of the Grammy award for musical excellence.

NARM—National Association of Record Manufacturers—Trade association whose membership includes rack jobbers, retail outlets, and record manufacturing companies which include major record corporations.

NATRA—National Association of Television and Radio Artists—An industry trade association whose membership includes the minority.

Needle Drop—a fee assessed by music suppliers for using their music as background.

NMPA—National Music Publishers Association.

O

One Stop—A sub-distributor whose clients are usually smaller record retail outlets and jukebox operators.

P

P. and D.—Pressing and Distribution—An arrangement between large and small companies wherein the large company will provide these services to the smaller one for a fee.

Payola—The illegal giving or receiving of any gratuity to obtain favorable radio or television airplay.

Polyvinyl Choloride (PVC)—A petroleum derivative that serves as the raw material in the manufacturing of vinyl discs.

R

Rack Jobber—A music merchandiser responsible for selling records in non-music outlets. (i.e. variety stores)

R and B (radio)—Rhythm and Blues. A radio format designed to reach a predominately black audience. This format recognized by playlist of black artists performing music classified as blues and up tempo dance songs.

R and B (records)—An archaic classification of music recorded by black entertainers intended for, primarily, a black audience.

R & R—Radio and Records; An industry trade publication.

Record Awards—Gold and Platinum plaques given to represent sales milestones. Gold represents sales of 500,000 album units, 1,000,000 single units; Platinum status represents sales of 1,000,000 album units; 2,000,000 single units.

Returns—Unsold records or tapes sent back to manufacturers for cash credit to buyer's account.

RIAA—Recording Industry Association of America—Trade association whose members include major record companies. RIAA sets technical standards for the industry as well as certify record sales for Gold and Platinum awards.

Royalties—A contractual payment to an artist or producer representing a percentage of all actual record sales

S

Sampling—An electronic digital process in which an original analog sound is converted to a binary code for later playback in an electronic storage device.

SAG. Screen Actor's Guild—Trade union representing performers in motion pictures.

Scale—a fee assessed by unions on behalf of its members representing the minimum payment to be charged for work.

SESAC, Inc.—The third oldest American performing rights organization.

T

Top 40—A dated radio music programming technique wherein a station restricts the records it plays to a limited number—forty records—with each record given exposure based upon its relative popularity.

U

Urban Contemporary—A radio format designed to reach, primarily, a Black audience. (see R and B)

UPC—Universal Product Code. An identifying marking on packaging which is used by digital scanning devices for inventory control.

W

Wholesale—The price manufacturers charge for a product to its distributors. This price represents the manufacturers expense in producing the product plus a profit.

Y

YBPC—Young Black Programmers Coalition—Southern Regional trade organization representing minority broadcasters.

Appendix C

Directory of Record Cos.

Academy of Country Music
6255 Sunset Blvd. #915
Hollywood, CA 90028
(213) 462–2351

Accelerated Movement
17357 Tribune Street
Granada Hills, CA 91344

Ace of Hearts Records
P.O. Box 579, Kenmore Station
Boston, MA 02215
(617) 536–1770

Advanced Alternative Media
277 Church Street-3rd Floor
New York NY 10013

A.D. Muscolo Promotions
17357 Tribune Street
Granada Hills, CA 91344
(818) 366–0044

Allied Artists Records
11330 Ventura Blvd.
Studio City, CA 91604
(818) 506–3600

Alligator Records
P.O. Box 60234
Chicago, IL 60660

Alpine Records
1025 17th Ave. South
Nashville, TN 37212

Alpha Video/AMI Records
915 W. Main Street
Hendersonville, TN 37075

Alternative Tentacles
P.O. Box 11458
San Francisco, CA 94101
(415) 863–9292

A&M Records
1416 North La Brea
Los Angeles, CA 90028
(213) 469–2411
New Jersey Branch:
50 East Palisades Ave.
Englewood, NJ 07631
(201) 569–2727
New York Branch:
595 Madison Avenue
New York, NY 10022
(212) 846–0477

Don Anti Promotions
6628 Farralone Ave.
Canoga Park, CA 91303
(818) 716–9818

*Excerpted From pages 63–77 of the *Directory of Media Professionals* as of January 15, 1987.

Arista Records, Inc.
6 West 57th Street
New York, NY 10019
(212) 489–7400

Aspen Record Group
525 Brannan Street
San Francisco, CA 94107
(415) 974–3500

Atco Records
75 Rockefeller Plaza
New York, NY 10019
(212) 484–6400

Atlantic Records
75 Rockefeller Plaza
New York, NY 10019
(212) 484–6000

Attic Records Limited
624 King Street West, 3rd Floor
Toronto, Ontario, Canada
M5V 1M7

Big Time Records
6777 Hollywood Blvd., 7th Floor
Hollywood, CA 90028
(213) 460–4033

Capitol Records
1750 North Vine
Hollywood, CA 90028
(213) 462–6252
(213) 467–6550
(213) 757–7470

CBS Records Country
34 Music Square East
Nashville, TN 37203
(615) 742–4321

CBT Records
3318 E SSW Loop 323
Tyler, TX 75701
(214) 581–9945

CD Presents
1230 Grant Ave. Suite 531
San Francisco, CA 94133

Celluloid/Moving Target
330 Hudson Street
New York, NY 10013
(212) 741–8310

Century 21 Programming
4340 Beltwood Parkway
Dallas, TX 75244–3225
(800) 582–2100
(214) 934–2121

Chameleon Music Group
3355 W. El Segundo Blvd.
Hawthorne, CA 90250
(213) 973–8282

Chrysalis Records
645 Madison Avenue
New York, NY 10022
(212) 758–3555
1–800–221–8787

Linda Clark & Associates
P.O. Box 1304
Burbank, CA 91507
(818) 848–4058

Columbia Records
51 West 52nd Street
New York, NY 10019
(212) 975–4321

Country Music Association, Inc.
Seven Music Circle No.
Nashville, TN 37202
(615) 244–2840

Coyote Records
P.O. Box 112
Upper Hoboken, NJ 07030

Critique Records, Inc.
400 Main Street
Reading, MA 01867

DB Records
450 14th Street Suite 201 NW
Atlanta, GA 30318
(404) 521-3008

Drake-Chenault Enterprises, Inc.
2000 Randolph Rd. S.E.
Albuquerque, NM 87106
(800) 247-3303

Elektra
75 Rockefeller Plaza
New York, NY 10019
(212) 484-7214

EMI America Records
6920 Sunset Blvd.
Los Angeles, CA 90028
(213) 461-9141

EMI-America Country
(*See Capitol Country*)

Enigma Records
1750 East Holly Ave.
El Segundo, CA 90245
(213) 640-6869

E/P/A Records
51 West 52nd Street
New York, NY 10019
(212) 975-4321

Fun Stuff
3960 Laurel Canyon Blvd. #429
Studio City, CA 91604
(818) 762-3321

Geffen Records
9130 Sunset Blvd.
Los Angeles, CA 90069
(213) 278-9010

GRP Records
555 West 57th Street
New York, NY 10019

IRS Records
100 Universal City Plaza
Universal City, CA 91608
(818) 777-4730
New York Branch:
445 Park Ave., 6th Floor
New York, NY 10022
(212) 605-0601

Island Records
14 East 4th Street
New York, NY 10012
(212) 477-8000

Manhattan Records
1370 Avenue of the Americas
New York, NY 10019
(212) 757-7470

MCA Records
70 Universal City Plaza
Universal City, CA 91608
(818) 7770-4000

Modern Records
9111 Sunset Blvd.
Los Angeles, CA 90069
(213) 273-8111

Motown Records
6255 Sunset Blvd.
Hollywood, CA 90028
(213) 468-3500

MTM Records
21 Music Square E.
Nashville, TN 37203
(615) 242-1931

Music West
3140 Kerner Suite F
San Rafael, CA 94901
(415) 459-6000

Palo Alto/TBA Records
11026 Ventura Blvd. #2
Studio City, CA 91604
(213) 877-5106

Polygram Records
810 Seventh Ave.
New York, NY 10019
(212) 333–8000
Los Angeles Branch:
8355 Sunset Blvd., 3rd Floor
Los Angeles, CA 90069
(213) 656–3003
Nashville Branch:
10 Music Circle Sq.
Nashville, TN 37203
(615) 244–3776

Profile Records
740 Broadway, 7th Floor
New York, NY 10003
(212) 529–2600

Record Research Inc.
P.O. Box 200
Menomonee Falls, WI 53051

RCA Records
1133 Avenue of the Americas
New York, NY 10036
(212) 930–4000

Reptile Records
P.O. Box 121213
Nashville, TN 37212
(615) 329–0856

Restless/Pink Dust Records
1750 East Holly Ave.
El Segundo, CA 90245
(213) 640–3772

Rhino Records
1201 Olympic Blvd.
Santa Monica, CA 90404
(213) 450–6323

Scotti Brothers Records, Inc.
2114 Pico Blvd.
Santa Monica, CA 90405
(213) 450–3193

Slash Records
P.O. Box 48888
Los Angeles, CA 90048
(213) 937–4660

Sleeping Bag/Fresh Records
1974 Broadway
New York, NY 10023
(212) 724–1440
(212) 580–1717

Tommy Boy Records
1747 First Ave.
New York, NY 10128
(212) 722–2211

TVT Records
636 Avenue of Americas
Square West 19th Street
New York, NY 10011
(212) 929–0570

Twin/Tone Records
2541 Nicollet Avenue South
Minneapolis, MN 55404
(612) 872–0646

United Artists Records
450 N. Roxbury Drive
Beverly Hills, CA 90210
(213) 281–4140

Virgin Records
9247 Alden Drive
Beverly Hills, CA 90210
(213) 278–1181

Warner Brothers Records
3300 Warner Blvd.
Burbank, CA 91510
(818) 846–9090

The Welk Music Group
54 Music Square EAst
Nashville, TN 37203
(615) 256–7648

Westwood One
9540 Washington Blvd.
Culver City, CA 90232
(213) 204 5000

Windham Hill Productions
1416 North La Brea Avenue
Hollywood, CA 90028
(213) 469–2411

Wind and Sand Records
50 West 34th Street, Suite 11C5-PM
New York, NY 10001
(212) 279–9596

Paul Yeskel Promotions
33 Tenafly Road
Tenafly, NJ 07670
(201) 567–5931